INITIAL PUBLIC OFFERINGS: FINDINGS AND THEORIES

Innovations in Financial Markets and Institutions

Editors:

Robert Eisenbeis and Richard W. McEnally
University of North Carolina at Chapel Hill
Chapel Hill, North Carolina, U. S. A.

Other books in the series:

England, C. and Huertas, T.:
The Financial Services Revolution

Gup, B.:
Bank Mergers: Current Issues and Perspectives

Kormendi, R., Bernard, V., Pirrong, S., Snyder, E.:
Crises Resolution in the Thrift Industry

Hancock, D.:
A Theory of Production for the Financial Firm

England, C.:
Governing Banking's Future

Kaufman, G.:
Banking Structures in Major Countries

Anderson, S., and Born, J.:
Closed-End Investment Companies

INITIAL PUBLIC OFFERINGS:
FINDINGS AND THEORIES

Seth C. Anderson
University of North Florida

T. Randolph Beard
Auburn University

Jeffery A. Born
Northeastern University

Kluwer Academic Publishers
Boston / Dordrecht / London

Distributors for North America:
Kluwer Academic Publishers
101 Philip Drive
Assinippi Park
Norwell, Massachusetts 02061 USA

Distributors for all other countries:
Kluwer Academic Publishers Group
Distribution Centre
Post Office Box 322
3300 AH Dordrecht, THE NETHERLANDS

Library of Congress Cataloging-in-Publication Data
Anderson, Seth C.
    Initial public offerings : findings and theories / Seth C.
  Anderson, T. Randolph Beard, Jeffery A. Born.
        p.   cm. -- (Innovations in financial markets and institutions)
    Includes bibliographical references and index.
    ISBN 0-7923-9633-2
    1. Going public (Securities)   I. Beard, T. Randolph (Thomas
  Randolph) II. Born, Jeffery A.   III. Title.   IV. Series.
  HG4028.S7A53   1995
  658.15'224--dc20   95-37158
                                                              CIP

Printed on acid-free paper.

Printed in the United States of America

DEDICATION

This book is dedicated to our wives: Linda Anderson, Leslie Beard, and Mary Ann Born.

Contents

PREFACE

Initial public offerings (IPOs) play a crucial role in allocating resources in market economies. Because of the enormous importance of IPOs, understanding how IPOs work is fundamental in understanding financial markets generally. Of particular interest is the puzzling existence of high initial returns to equity IPOs in the United States and other free-market economies. This book is designed for use by anyone wishing to perform further academic research in the area of IPOs and by those practitioners interested in IPOs as investment vehicles.

In the book, we first give a brief overview of IPOs in the United States. This overview is followed by a concise treatment of IPOs' history, regulation, and process. Next we present summaries of academic articles' empirical findings on IPO returns. Chapter 4 presents theoretical models of IPOs and is followed by Chapter 5, which summarizes the findings of various tests of theories of underpricing. Chapter 6 is a brief conclusion.

We wish to express appreciation to Professors Robert Eisenbeis and Richard McEnally of the University of North Carolina, who made many helpful comments and who supported our writing a monograph in this area. We also thank Zachery Rolnik and the other editors of Kluwer for their helpful comments. The completion of the book was greatly facilitated by both Jeanne Davis and Cathy Kruse, who word-processed the manuscript and by Linda Anderson, who edited it. We thank our patient wives and families for their moral support.

IPO WORKS SUMMARIZED
IN THIS MONOGRAPH

1. INITIAL PUBLIC OFFERINGS: AN INTRODUCTION

An Initial Public Offering (IPO) comprises a private firm's accessing the public capital market through the sale of securities. Thereby, the firm can raise monies more readily than by the retention of profits. Other possible motivations for an IPO include the prestige of ownership of a public company or the desire of major shareholders to exit the company.

The corporation can raise this external capital by selling a variety of different securities -- primarily different types of bonds, common stock, and preferred stock. Figure 1 depicts the growth of the sale of the securities over the period 1938 through 1993.

Interestingly, the relative importance of the three primary types of security issuance has changed over the half century. Figure 2 shows that the issuance of common shares in the 1990-1993 period comprises 13.26% of total offerings, compared with 4.93% in the 1938-1941 period. Preferred offerings constitute roughly one-half of their relative position today compared with the earlier period. Preferred share offerings dominated common offerings in the earlier period; whereas today common offerings dominate preferred offerings.[1]

This obviously important economic process has over the past three decades generated a plethora of academic studies investigating various aspects of the process. The preponderance of these works has addressed the pricing and price behavior of these new securities. Generally, the studies have focused on common stocks, and only a few have involved bonds and preferred stocks.

The purpose of this monograph is to present the findings and theories reported in more than seventy studies published in the last thirty years. These studies comprise those most frequently cited in the academic literature.

Figure 1
Initial Public Offferings*

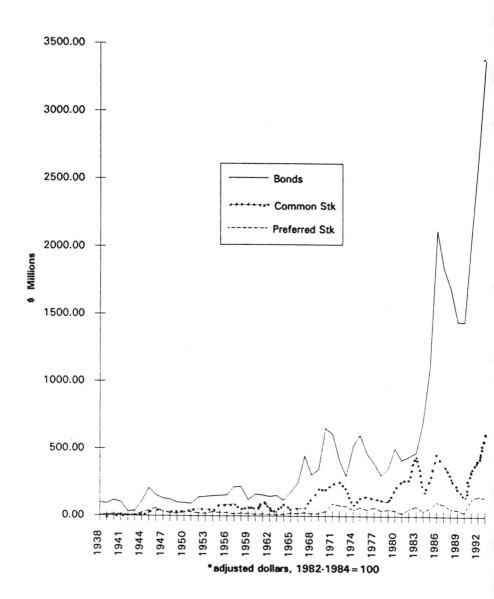

*adjusted dollars, 1982-1984 = 100

Figure 2

Common Stock, Preferred Stock, and Bond Offerings

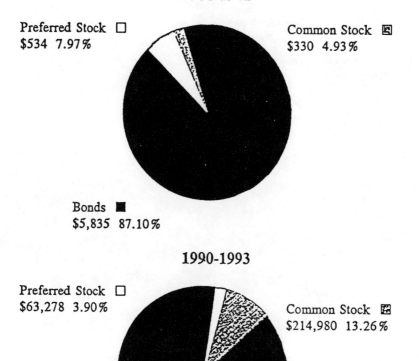

1938-1941

Preferred Stock ☐
$534 7.97%

Common Stock ▣
$330 4.93%

Bonds ■
$5,835 87.10%

1990-1993

Preferred Stock ☐
$63,278 3.90%

Common Stock ▣
$214,980 13.26%

Bonds ■
$1,342,674 82.83%

In Chapter 2 we present an overview of the history, regulation and process of IPOs in the United States. Chapter 3 gives a brief summary of the empirical findings of various IPO studies investigating the price behavior of new offerings. In Chapter 4 we review the theories which have been posited for the pricing of IPOs. The economic theories include adverse selection, principal-agent, signalling, and those we include as "heterodox explanations." Chapter 5 presents the results of tests for explanations of underpricing. Our conclusions and some suggestions for further analysis are given in Chapter 6.

2. HISTORY, REGULATION, AND PROCESS

To effect an IPO in modern times the private company must seek permission from the Securities and Exchange Commission (SEC). In administering the Securities Act of 1933, the SEC requires the selling company to publicly disclose pertinent facts about the firm's business, current operations, management, primary shareholders, and financial condition. Before the regulation and process of a current-day IPO is considered, a brief review of early IPOs may be appropriate.

INITIAL PUBLIC OFFERINGS: EARLY YEARS

During the early 1800's in the United States conventional securities which were traded on the exchanges primarily comprised government bonds and insurance and bank stocks.[2] Activity on the securities exchanges grew slowly until the 1830's, when the development of commercial railroads required more financing.[3] Early in the decade, new firms raised monies by using the services of promoters who opened subscription books and sold common shares to the public -- friends, relatives, and businessmen[4] Initially the strong demand for railroad shares resulted in oversubscription. After a few years the sale of stocks required more effort than previously. Promoters aggressively marketed common shares through public meetings, parades, and door-to-door canvassing, making the potential railroad's communities aware of the benefits they would reap from being on a line. Sales of common stock were strong, but not strong enough. The evolving industry's vast demand for money ultimately resulted in the development of new financial instruments, such as various classes of preferred stock and mortgage bonds. "The concept met with success: securities tailored to different risk preferences attracted wider sources of funds, and the capital formation potential of the corporate system was greatly enlarged."[5] Trading activity in railroad securities expanded rapidly into the second half of the nineteenth century.

During and after the Civil War, Jay Cooke used his own techniques and the French syndicate method to sell government securities and Northern Pacific Railroad bonds in European markets. Under the French syndicate method the manager for a group of bankers would arrange a loan at a large bank or trust company. The debt would be backed by securities of the company seeking funds. These securities would be sold and the loan retired. If security sales failed to reach expectations, the members of the bankers' group were responsible for losses. This method allowed a company to get funds before securities were sold. Cooke failed in the Depression of 1873, owing to over-extension on Northern Pacific Railroad commitments, but his techniques survived and thrived[6]

During the decades following the Civil War, public awareness of stocks increased substantially, relative to earlier in the century. This was due to increased securities issuance and to changes in technology. Stock tickers were adopted in 1867, and the telephone debuted in 1878. By the late 1870's New York Stock Exchange (NYSE) trading volume had grown to approximately 80,000 shares per session, compared to 5,000-10,000 share sessions on the NYSE's predecessor fifty years earlier.[7]

The first investment banking firm, Harris, Forbes, originated in Chicago in 1880. This firm bought entire issues of a company's stock and sold these securities to institutions and individual investors[8] As this practice of underwriting evolved, the role of promoters diminished. Securities sales became more organized and sophisticated. Evidence was J.P. Morgan & Co.'s successful syndication in 1901, which raised $1.5 billion to conglomerate several small steel firms into the United States Steel Company.[9] By this time shares in industrial firms were widely held and traded. Daily volume on the NYSE often exceeded one million shares.

Around the turn of the century public concern over big business activities resulted in federal regulations, such as:

1.) The Act to Regulate Commerce (1887), which applied to railroads,

2.) The Sherman Antitrust Act (1890), which dealt with trade restraint, and

3.) The Clayton and Federal Trade Commission Acts (1914), which supplemented the Sherman Act.[10]

Interestingly, after 1910 it was at the state level, not the federal level, where the regulation of securities sales began to appear. Companies wishing to make an initial public offering were required to file with the appropriate authority in their state of incorporation. The general purpose for this filing was to protect investors, as best possible, from buying a piece of a "blue sky" -- hence the term "blue sky", which survives until today.[11] For example, with the 1913 Florida Statutes:

> "the law provided that investment companies were required to file specific information with the Comptroller prior to the sale of securities products. The information to be filed included a detailed statement of the plan on which it was proposing to transact business, a copy of all stocks, bonds, products to be offered for sale, an itemized account of the company's financial standing, and written consent that it would accept court interference if a cause for action should arise."[12]

Various states employed different agencies and agency structures for filings.

Before 1900 the chief securities which traded on the exchanges were state, municipal and federal bonds, and railroad securities. By 1914 public utility and industrial stocks took the lead. Total volume often saw a three-million-share day.[13] In 1920 the NYSE witnessed the trading of 227 million shares and bond volume of $3.9 billion. As the decade passed, share volume grew to 1.13 billion, but bond volume declined to $3.0 billion in 1929.[14] During the 1920's share prices soared, partially because of an expanding economy and profits. Another driving force was the funds supplied by brokers and/or banks for the purchase of securities in margin accounts. The common downpayment in a margin account was between 10% and 25%.[15] Concomitantly, investors lost approximately $25 billion through the purchase of worthless securities between 1923 and 1929.[16]

Through affiliate operations there were interlocking directorates among banks, and banks participated in underwriting and distributing corporate bonds.[17] After the market crashed in 1929, activities of commercial banks and securities firms came to be scrutinized by Congress. As the Depression set in, the banking system suffered massive failures at least partially caused by abuses. Many thought that further restraints in the banking and securities industry were needed. The Banking Act of 1933, known as the Glass-Steagall Act, was enacted to stop abusive banking practices by restructuring the banking industry. With the mood of the times, abuses in the securities world, per se, were addressed by two primary acts: the Securities Act of 1933 and the Securities and Exchange Act of 1934.

REGULATION AND PROCESS

Regulation
The Securities Act of 1933 (often referred to as the Truth in Securities Act) was a response to the public outcry following the widespread investment and securities abuses of the roaring 1920's. To quote, this was:

> "An Act to provide full and fair disclosure of the character of securities sold in interstate and foreign

commerce and through the mails, and to prevent frauds in the sale thereof, and for other purposes."[18]

In this Act firms wishing to raise capital via an IPO were required to file proper documents with the Federal Trade Commission (hereafter Commission). The primary characteristics of the 1933 Act are well summarized by Schwartz:[19]

"The Securities Act of 1933 (The 1933 Act):

- Mandated disclosure of information about new corporate securities
- Required that all new corporate securities be registered with the Federal Trade Commission (later with the Securities and Exchange Commission)
- Demanded that financial information in a registration statement be certified by an independent accountant
- Stipulated antifraud provisions."

The 1933 Act challenged the principle of caveat emptor, which was manifest in the securities market previously. The burden of telling the truth resided with the sellers of shares (the issuing companies).[20] The act gave investors the right to file suit to recover financial losses resulting from incorrect, distorted, or omitted information in the offering material required by the Act.[21]

Following the 1933 Act, Congress passed the Securities Exchange Act of 1934, which established further regulatory and administrative control of the securities markets. The Act's objectives were:

"to provide for the regulation of securities exchanges and of over-the-counter markets operating in interstate and foreign commerce and through the mails, to prevent inequitable and unfair practices on such exchanges and markets, and for other purposes."[22]

Again, from Schwartz, the primary characteristics of the 1934 Act are summarized:[23]

"The Securities Exchange Act of 1934 (The 1934 Act):

- Extended disclosure requirements established by the 1933 Act to existing securities
- Established the Securities and Exchange Commission (SEC)
- Empowered the SEC to approve commission rates changes proposed by the exchanges and to request commission rate changes
- Empowered the SEC to change rules, to prohibit stock manipulation, and to formulate additional regulations as necessary
- Established regulation of the business conduct of broker/dealer members of an exchange
- Left disciplinary power over its members to the exchanges
- Empowered the Federal Reserve Board to set minimum margin requirements."

In essence, the 1933 and 1934 Acts were responses to the need for increasing the flow of corporate information from new and existing firms, respectively, to the capital market. Other acts, such as the Maloney Act of 1938, the Investment Company Act of 1940, the Securities Investor Protection Act of 1970, etc., are beyond the scope of this monograph.

Process

Once management decides to pursue an IPO, the process can take as little as six months or up to approximately two years, depending on circumstances. The firm must decide whether to pursue a full registration, a simplified registration, or an exempt registration. Simplified and exempt registrations require less disclosure and involve smaller offerings than most full registrations, which usually are done with an investment banker's services. The preliminary offer structure and the offering valuation are arrived at by management and an underwriter who has expertise in this area. The underwriter works with SEC counsel in complying with state and federal rules. The registration statement, consisting of a prospectus and any other materials, is filed with the SEC. The prospectus is a booklet containing all significant negative and positive information about the company and those involved with the company. The SEC's Department of Corporate Finance reviews the statement to determine any misstatements or omissions. If there are no problems, the statement becomes effective after 20 days.

When the statement is filed, the managing underwriter begins forming a syndicate of other underwriters and broker-dealers who will participate in the offering. Once the syndicate is formed, retail brokers can distribute the preliminary prospectus and solicit interest in the offer from their clients.

On the afternoon prior to the offering date's becoming effective, after the market closes, management and the underwriter meet to set the final price and number of shares to be sold. Heretofore, the underwriter and management had been working under a letter of intent. The following morning the underwriting agreement is finalized among management and all underwriting parties. As soon as this occurs, a pricing amendment giving final details of the offering is sent to the SEC. The selling begins, and the final prospectus is printed. The offering's closing day is stipulated in the underwriting agreement, and the underwriter must abide. On this date management and the lead underwriter meet and swap stock certificates for a check.

Many think that, ideally, the price of the new stock in the secondary market should remain near the offering price. Often this is not the case. Some issues are stabilized by the underwriter at a price equal to or slightly below the offering price. Other IPO issues are strongly demanded and exhibit large first-day gains.

These apparent mis-pricings have long intrigued practitioners and academicians alike. A large body of literature has grown from studies researching the issue of IPO price behavior and theorizing as to the determinants of this behavior.

In the following chapter we present a brief summary of many of those empirical articles which show the apparent mis-pricings having been investigated over the past three decades. Subsequent chapters summarize and analyze various economic models offered to explain IPO price behavior.

3. EMPIRICAL FINDINGS

Early IPO studies primarily describe and develop series of stylized facts about new issues' price performance. This performance appears to be anomalous and not easily explainable using theories at that time. In particular the studies report evidence of consistent underpricing of new issues resulting in significant short-term returns which often evaporate over time. Such results are inconsistent with efficient markets and with effective information processing by underwriters and buyers of new issues. These early findings stimulated the writing of theoretical papers attempting to explain IPO price behavior and to test the models empirically.

In this chapter we summarize these early descriptive studies and describe their initial conclusions. Chapter 4 gives a presentation of theoretical works attempting to explain IPO pricing behavior. Chapter 5 contains empirical tests of these models.

The papers below are categorized as: (1) Domestic Common Stock, (2) Foreign Common Stock, (3) Bonds, and (4) Investment Company/Other Offerings. Table 3.1 gives an alphabetical listing by author and has statistics on securities offered (offer), sample size (size), sample period (years), offering type (type), initial returns (return), return period (S/L), and sample price/value constraint (value).

DOMESTIC COMMON STOCK

In "Investors' Experience With New Stock Issues" Reilly and Hatfield in 1969 use 53 IPOs for the 12/63-6/65 period. They report an average 9.9% return from offering price to first market price. They find that during this period new issue price changes are more variable than price changes for the OTC Industrials Average and the Dow Jones Industrials Average. The strong returns persist up to one year after the IPO.

TABLE 3.1
SUMMARY OF EMPIRICAL FINDINGS

DATE	AUTHORS*	OFFER**	SIZE	YEAR	TYPE	RETURN %	S/L	VALUE
1993	Affleck-Graves, et al.	CS	1127	83-87	F	4.82 - 10.4	S	> $1
1993	Aggarwal, et al.	CS	142	80-90	X	2.8 - 78.5	S, L	X
1990	Aggarwal & Rivoli	CS	1598	77-87	F	10.7	S, L	Exc. Reg A
1991	Aggarwal & Rivoli	CS	1556,296	77-87	F, BE	9.9 - 51.7	S	Exc. Reg A
1989	Anderson & Born	CS	35	86-87	F	Neg	S, L	X
1992	Anderson & Born	CS	30	86-89	F	Neg	S, L	X
1991	Anderson, Born & Beard	CS	43	70-87	F	Neg	S, L	X
1988	Balvers, et al.	CS	1182	81-85	F	7.84	S	> $1
1993	Barry & Jennings	CS	229	88-90	F	6.1	S	> $1
1975	Bear & Curley [4,5]	CS	140	1969	X	9.5	S, L	> $450,000
1986	Beatty & Ritter [4,5]	CS	1028	77-82	F, BE	Positive	S	Exc. Reg A
1980	Block & Stanley	CS	102	74-78	X	5.96	S, L	X
1981	Buckland, et al.	CS	297	65-75	X	27	S	X
1990	Carter & Manaster [4,5]	CS	501	79-83	F	13.1 - 19.56	S	> $2 Mil
1987	Chalk & Peavy [5]	CS	649	75-82	F, BE	19.6 - 37.8	S, L	NO

Table 3.1 - Summary of Empirical Findings - Continued

DATE	AUTHORS*	OFFER**	SIZE	YEAR	TYPE	RETURN %	S/L	VALUE
1992	Cho	CS	717	75-84	BE	42.3	S	X
1982	Downes & Heinkel [5]	CS	449	65-69	F	X	X	Exc. Reg A
1993	Drake & Vetsuypens	CS	93	69-90	X	9.18	S, L	X
1974	Ederington [5]	B	611	64-71	X	X	X	X
1986	Fung & Rudd	B	123	83-85	X	X	X	X
1975	Ibbotson & Jaffe [4,5]	CS	128	60-70	X	16.8	S	X
1988	Ibbotson, et al. [5]	CS	2439	75-84	F	8.6 - 42.8	S	Exc. Reg A
1975	Ibbotson [4,5]	CS	120	60-69	X	11.4	S	X
1987	Jog & Riding	CS	100	71-83	X	9 - 11.5	S	X
1988	Johnson & Miller [4,5]	CS	502	81-83	F	11.2 - 14	S	Exc. Reg A
1989	Koh & Walter [4,5]	CS	66	73-87	X	11.2 -14	S	X
1993	Levis	CS	712	80-88	F, BE	14.3?	S, L	X
1977	Lindvall	B	120	63-72	X	X	X	X
1991	Loderer, et al.	PS	251	80-84	F	Neg	X	X
1973	Logue	CS	250	65-69	F	20.8 - 52.1	X	Exc. Reg A

Table 3.1 - Summary of Empirical Findings - Continued

DATE	AUTHORS*	OFFER**	SIZE	YEAR	TYPE	RETURN %	S/L	VALUE
1989	McBain & Krause	CS	759	78-85	F	X	S	X
1972	McDonald & Fisher	CS	142	69-70	X	28.5	S, L	>$1 Mil
1974	McDonald & Jacquillat	CS	31	68-71	X	3	S	X
1992	Mauer & Senbet [4,5]	CS	1002	77-84	F	18.9	S	Exc. Reg A
1991	Megginson & Weiss [4]	CS	640	83-87	F	7.1 - 11.9	S	>$3 Mil
1987	Miller & Reilly [5]	CS	510	82-83	X	9.9	S	Exc. Reg A
1988	Muscarella	LP	50	83-87	X	0	S	X
1989	Muscarella & Vetsuypen [4,5]	CS	38	70-87	F, BE	7.12	S	X
1974	Neuberger & Hammond	CS	816	65-69	X	17	S, L	Exc. Reg A
1983	Neuberger & LaChapell	CS	118	75-80	X	8.3 - 73.5	S, L	X
1983	Peavy	CS	41	85-87	F	Neg	S, L	X
1973	Reilly	CS	53	63-65	X	9.9 - 43.7	S, L	X
1977	Reilly	CS	553	72-75	X	10.8	S, L	NO
1969	Reilly & Hatfield	CS	53	63-65	X	18.3 - 20.2	S, L	X

Table 3.1 - Summary of Empirical Findings - Continued

DATE	AUTHORS*	OFFER**	SIZE	YEAR	TYPE	RETURN %	S/L	VALUE
1984	Ritter [4,5]	CS	1028	77-82	X	16.3 - 48.4	S	Exc. Reg A
1984	Ritter [4,5]	CS	559	65-73	X	X	X	Sales > $1 Mil
1991	Ritter	CS	1526	75-84	X	14.3 - 17	S, L	>$1 SH > $1 Mil
1970	Stoll & Curley	CS	205	57, 59, 63	X	42.4 - 75	S, L	Reg A Only
1988	Tinic [4,5]	CS	204	23-71	X	5.1 - 14.2	S	$5 SH > $0.5 Mil
1992	Wang, Chen & Gau	REIT	87	71-88	X	-2.8	S	X
1978	Weinstein	B	179	62-74	X	0	S	X
1989	Weiss	CS	64	85-87	F	0	S, L	X

*   4 and 5 = chapter numbers.
**   CS = Common Stock, PS = Preferred Stock, B = Bonds.
X   = not specified
F   = Firm commitment
BE = Best efforts
S   = short-term returns
L   = long-term returns

Next, Stoll and Curley present an empirical study of the adequacy of outside equity as a source of funds.[24] Utilizing a sample of 643 Regulation A offerings during 1957, 1959, and 1963, the authors compute both initial and long-term returns. They report a market-adjusted return of 42.4% initially. However, they also report that over subsequent six-month intervals these shares generally experience negative returns sufficient to more than offset the initial short-run price surge.[25]

Following Stoll and Curley, the next primarily empirical work is that of McDonald and Fisher in 1972, who find that early IPO price behavior has no value in predicting later return behavior for these issues. The authors compute market-adjusted returns for 142 unseasoned equity IPOs over five different time periods ranging from "offering to first week" to "offering to one year." Each offering is made in the first quarter of 1969. They conclude that markets are efficient because subsequent returns from the end of the first week are not different for high-return IPOs.

In a 1973 article entitled "On the Pricing of Unseasoned Equity Issues: 1965-1969," Logue posits a monopsony model wherein the underwriter's purchase price is a function of the relative bargaining power of the underwriter and the issuer.

The model is tested using a final sample of 250 IPOs from the 3/65 - 2/69 period. Most variables have the hypothesized sign. Market ebullience, value, and secondary variables each have statistical significance. In a second test an underwriter prestige variable has significance. The authors conclude that the differences in the performance of prestigious and less prestigious offerings could be explained in part by differences in the issues themselves.

In a follow-up study to Reilly and Hatfield, Reilly in 1973 investigates IPO short-run returns in the declining market beginning in 1966. Using a sample of 62 IPOs, Reilly compares the first year's returns for IPOs in both their earlier study and this one during a declining market environment. He finds that the market-adjusted returns are significant during the weak market period, but their magnitude is reduced from those experienced in the earlier study.

In the 1974 article "A Study of Underwriters' Experience With Unseasoned New Issues," Neuberger and Hammond address whether there is a difference in the pricing behavior by individual underwriters. Using a sample of 48 underwriters meeting specific criteria, the authors select 816 new issues for examination. They find a significant difference in the returns to underwriters' portfolios from the date of issue to one week or one month later. The authors conclude that secondary issues appreciate less than primary issues. Also, non-prestigious underwriters' portfolios appreciate more than those of prestigious underwriters.

Reilly in the 1977 article "New Issues Revisited," utilizes a sample of 553 new stock offerings for the 1972-1975 period and measures price changes for several periods. Among the periods are: from offering to first Wednesday after offering, from offering to fourth Wednesday after offering, and from offering to year after offering. His findings are in agreement with earlier studies and comprise initial excess returns in the 11% range.

In a 1980 article, Block and Stanley examine 204 IPOs made during the 1969-1972 and the 1974-1978 periods. They report short-term excess returns which are more positive for the offerings of non-prestigious underwriters. Longer-term returns are found to be less positive than the mean 5.96% first-week excess return during the 1974-1978 period.

The following year Neuberger and LaChapelle in "Unseasoned New Issue Price Performance on Three Tiers: 1975-1980," investigate whether or not there is a difference in the pricing policies of three different underwriter classes. They define three tiers of underwriters consistent with the Hayes hierarchies and employ a sample of 118 new issues for the 7/70 through 6/80 period to compute excess returns for six periods ranging from "offer to one week" to "one month after-offer to six months after-offer." It is found that mean excess returns generally increase as underwriter prestige decreases.

In 1988 "Underpricing of New Issues and the Choice of Auditor as a Signal of Investment Banker Reputation" by Balvers, McDonald, and Miller examines a sample of 1,182 IPOs offered by 181 different investment banking firms. They find that high reputation investment bankers tend to select high reputation auditors. Also, they report that offerings by high reputation investment bankers are underpriced less than offerings by other investment bankers.

McBain and Krause in 1989 employ a sample of 759 for the period 1/78 to 8/85 to investigate the issue of insiders' retention on IPOs' values. They find that larger relative valuations are experienced by firms in which insiders maintain larger relative holdings. They also report a positive relationship between offering P/E ratio and degree of insider ownership.

In a 1990 work "Fads in the Initial Public Offering Market," Aggarwal and Rivoli employ a sample of 1,598 offerings over the 1977-1987 period to investigate whether the price behavior of IPOs is consistent with the presence of fads. They find that early abnormal returns are significantly positive, but that prices decline significantly in the year following the initial offering. The phenomenon holds in groupings based on size, offering price, year, and underwriter class. They conclude that their findings are supportive of IPOs being subject to overvaluation or fads in early aftermarket trading.

In 1991 Aggarwal and Rivoli address the cost of going public using a sample of 1,556 firm commitment and 196 best-efforts offerings during the period 1977-1987. They address cash expenses, investment banking commissions, and underpricing. They find that total costs are more than three times higher for best efforts offerings than for firm commitments.

In "The Long Run Performance of Initial Public Offerings," Ritter employs a sample of 1,526 IPOs in 1975-1984. Using a 36-

month time frame, he reports that IPOs, on average, exhibit positive returns during the first two months, but returns become negative in the months that follow. He reports that investing in IPOs at the close of the first day of trading, then holding them for three years would leave the investor with 83 cents, compared to a dollar resulting from investing in matched firms on the American Stock Exchange and NYSE.

Cho uses a sample of 717 best-efforts offerings from 1975 to 1984 to test the signalling model of Welch in explaining best-efforts IPO offerings, incorporating the possibility of failure. He finds that the proportion of negative, zero, and positive initial returns is 18%, 18%, and 64%, respectively. On average the initial return is 42.3%. He concludes that the optimal offer price is determined by considering the trade-off between underpricing and the probability of failure.

In 1993 Drake and Vetsuypens focus primarily on 93 IPOs over the period 1969 to 1990 which were sued for misstatements in the IPO prospectus or registration statement under the 1933 or 1934 Federal Securities Acts. The suits followed large price declines. However, the authors report that the average first-day initial return for the sample was 9.18%.

Barry and Jennings employ initial-day opening prices for 229 IPOs during the period 12/88 - 12/90 to investigate IPOs' opening price performance. They find that the IPO offer-to-close return averages 6.78% for the full sample and that approximately 90% of this initial return is earned on the opening transaction. The subsequent return for the remainder of the day is less than the typical transaction cost. Essentially all of the initial return goes to the initial purchaser.

Lastly, Affleck-Graves, Hedge, Miller, and Reilly utilize a sample of 1,127 IPOs over the 1983-1987 period to investigate the effect of the trading system on the underpricing of IPOs. They find average first-day returns for the IPOs on the NYSE, AMEX, NASDAQ/NMS, and NASDAQ/non-MKS of 4.82%, 2.16%,

5.56%, and 10.41%, respectively. They conclude that these returns provide support for the certification proposition.

FOREIGN COMMON STOCK

McDonald and Jacquillat in the 1974 article "Pricing of Initial Equity Issues: The French Sealed-Bid Auction," analyze a sample of 31 new common stock issues in France for the 1968-71 period. Under the sealed-bid auction method they find the mean market-adjusted initial returns to successful bidders is 3.0%. This finding supports their hypothesis that initial prices are set several percentage points below market equilibrium prices and that the market adjustment subsequent to the issue is rapid.[26]

In 1981 Buckland, Herbert, and Yeomans use a sample of 297 IPOs made in the United Kingdom over the period 4/1/65 through 3/31/75. They report that new issues yield returns in excess of 20% over the first fourteen days of trading.

Jog and Riding in the 1987 article "Underpricing in Canadian IPOs" use a sample of 100 Canadian IPOs over the 1971-1983 period and find average initial three-day returns of 9% to 11.5%. They report that underpricing is significantly related to three variables: (1) trading volume, (2) industry sector, and (3) utilization of offering proceeds.

In the 1990 article "The Winner's Curse Problem, Interest Costs and the Underpricing of Initial Public Offerings," Levis utilizes a sample of 123 United Kingdom "Offers For Sale" new issues during the period January, 1985 to December, 1988. He finds that these issues had been sold at an average market-adjusted discount of 8.6%. He also reports that there is no significance between first day opening and closing raw returns.

Aggarwal, Leal, and Hernandez in 1993 examine a total of 142 IPOs in Brazil, Chile, and Mexico over the 1980-1990 period. The 1993 paper reports short-term returns of 78.5%, 16.7%, and 2.8%, respectively. Long-run returns are reported to be negative, which is consistent with long-run IPO price behavior in the United States.

Levis, also in 1993, utilizes 712 IPOs in the United Kingdom over the 1980-1988 period. He reports an average first-day return of 14.3%. The study also shows that these IPOs underperform other benchmarks in the three years following the initial offering.[27]

BONDS

In a 1977 article dealing with the yield spread between new and seasoned bonds, Lindvall hypothesizes that changes in seasoned yields lag changes in new issue yields owing to the institutional structure in the corporate bond market. The three hypotheses about why new issue rates might differ from seasoned rates are: (1) the bonds somehow differ; (2) the underwriters may intentionally misprice; and (3) the underwriters might unintentionally underprice. The author investigates various new issue and seasoned yield series and finds that seasoned yields lag changes in new issue yields. It is also found that new and newly issued bond trading volume exceeds seasoned bond trading volume. He concludes that the supply and demand for new issues is significant in determining interest rates.[28]

Weinstein in the 1978 work "The Seasoning Process of New Corporate Bond Issues" considers three hypotheses concerning the seasoning of new issue bonds: (1) there is no seasoning process whatsoever; (2) bonds are initially underpriced, but the underpricing quickly disappears; and (3) the seasoning process extends over months. He uses a sample of 179 new issues over the June, 1962 to July, 1974 period and finds that the new bonds are brought out at prices which allow an abnormal return of .383% over the first month. There are no abnormal returns over the ensuing months.

In a 1986 article Fung and Rudd address the pricing of new corporate bond issues. They obtain a sample of new issues for the period 1/83 to 10/85 from *Moody's*. Their findings are somewhat different from earlier ones. They conclude that there is no clear evidence of underpricing at the offer. They offer as a difference between their studies and earlier ones their use of trader quotes for pricing. They report that the impact of issue methods differs in high- versus low-yield market environments.

INVESTMENT COMPANY/OTHER OFFERINGS

In the 1988 work "Price Performance of Initial Public Offerings of Master Limited Partnership Units," Muscarella examines a sample of fifty master limited partnerships (MLPs) which occurred over the January, 1983 through July, 1987 period. In sharp contrast to other IPOs, the MLPs exhibit no significant underpricing. He concludes that the findings are consistent with security pricing in an efficient market.

Over the 1989-1992 period there are five articles which investigate the IPO price behavior of closed-end investment companies: studies by Weiss (1989); Anderson and Born (1989); Peavy (1990); Anderson, Born, and Beard (1991); and Anderson and Born (1992). These studies use various samples of investment company IPOs over varying periods in the 1970s and 1980s. Generally, the studies report little initial excess return and negative returns during the weeks following the offerings. The few offerings which do trade at premiums to the offering price are those of other-country funds.

Loderer, Sheehan, and Kadlec employ samples of 1,608 seasoned stock issues and 251 new issues of preferred stock in a 1991 article. They find that underwriters do not systematically set prices below market on the exchanges but often do so on NASDAQ. The new classes of preferred stock are not underpriced.

Wang, Chan, and Gau in the 1992 work "Initial Public Offerings of Equity Securities: Anomalous Evidence Using REITs" use a sample of 87 real estate investment trusts over the 1971-1988 period. They document an average initial-day return of -2.82%. They also report that the new REITs significantly underperform a matched sample of seasoned REITs over the 189 trading days following the offering date.

SUMMARY

From the above studies several conclusions about IPO initial return behavior can be drawn: (1) common stock IPOs both in the United States and internationally have experienced high initial returns; (2) the returns usually are inversely related to the "quality" of the offering as proxied by offering size and/or underwriter prestige; (3) bond, preferred stock, and limited partnership IPOs generally exhibit insignificant initial returns; and (4) closed-end investment company and REIT IPOs usually experience negative returns over their post-offering seasoning periods. The following chapter presents theoretical models of IPOs.

4. THEORETICAL MODELS OF IPOs

INTRODUCTION

The empirical analyses summarized in Chapter 3 point to several well-established facts about the characteristics of initial public offerings of stocks in the U. S. and other countries. While some of these facts are unsurprising (e.g., IPOs are risky), several features of IPO performance are startling and require some explanation. By far the most striking empirical finding on IPOs is a consistent pattern of excess returns on the first day of trading. While such returns clearly undergo secular movements in extent, timing, and duration, Ibbotson's (1975) finding of 11.4% average first day returns remains a plausible figure. Since aftermarket trading appears efficient, what factor or factors account for this extraordinary anomaly? When so much money is being "left on the table," one naturally asks "why?"

The large first day average returns to IPO equity securities caused considerable perplexity when they were first widely noted decades ago. Yet it was only with the development since the 1970s of sufficiently powerful analytic tools that "formal," i.e., theoretically rigorous, explanations of IPO behavior were proposed. Developments in game theory, financial economics, and information theory all contributed to the small "explosion" in theoretical analyses of IPOs observed since the early 1980s.

The formal or modern approach to modeling economic phenomena (such as IPO returns) is less a body of received theories than a discipline imposed on alleged explanations. Unlike earlier analyses of IPO returns that discussed such factors as "uncertainty" or "market ebullience," the modern approach pays great attention to describing the informational environment in which economic actors make transactions. All market participants are required to act with great cunning, and to decide their plans by engaging in calculations that may well be beyond the capacity of the analyst describing their behavior. Any sort of singular behavior -- such as might create excess returns in IPOs -- cannot be attributed to "mistakes" or erroneous beliefs by market participants. Instead the analyst must explain exactly how such strange behavior is actually consistent with the great sophistication of all market participants.[29]

Modern theories of IPO pricing offer various explanations for underpricing, and these explanations arise from important informational asymmetries between market participants. Since an IPO involves four relevant groups of actors -- the issuing firm, the underwriting/distribution syndicate, the initial buyers, and the larger set of investors in the secondary market -- the information known to these various groups is critical. Although agents can have different information without any agent having unambiguously superior information, most models of IPO pricing typically assume one group has superior information on firm value. Other agents know this (although they do not know exactly what the information is) and behave accordingly. Further, everyone knows that everyone knows this, and so on ad infinitum.[30]

The most widely discussed theories of IPO underpricing differ in their assumptions about which actors have superior information. Since offerings substantially vary in their sizes, terms, and market environments, it is perhaps unrealistic to expect that the informational assumptions in any one model will be applicable to all IPOs. Nevertheless, some assumptions are probably more realistic than others.

Although both the main modern and the "heterodox" models of IPO pricing will be described in this chapter, it is useful at this initial stage to examine the informational assumptions one might make. First, one could assume that the issuer has better information on security value than do the underwriters or investors. This assumption, which is consistent with so much of the contemporary literature on the agency theory of the firm, gives rise to "signalling" models of underpricing. In these scenarios, underpricing is paradoxically used as a convincing claim of good firm value. Issuers recoup the money they give away by benefiting from higher prices in a later, seasoned offering of additional shares.

Alternately, underwriters/distributors can be assumed to possess information superior to the issuer (and, perhaps, investors). This assumption leads naturally to the "principal-agent" models of the initial public offering. The underwriter has valuable, private information on market demand. The issuer will wish to learn this information, yet must offer an incentive to the underwriter to truthfully reveal it. Further, the success of the offer depends not just on market conditions, but also on underwriter effort which may itself be unobserved by the issuer. In order to secure truthful revelation of private information and encourage promotion efforts, the issuer may agree to a contract that leads to underpricing.

In contrast to the assumptions of the principal-agent and signalling models, the most important informational asymmetry may arise within a market group rather than between different groups. The assumption that, for example, a (potentially small) group of investors has information superior to that of other investors and the issuer gives rise to the "adverse selection" model of underpricing. In this formulation, the existence of investors with superior information about issue value places uninformed investors at a disadvantage. Uninformed investors face competition for good shares, but have a higher probability of obtaining bad shares due to the rationing mechanism applied to oversubscribed offerings. To induce the uninformed to participate in the IPO markets, shares must be underpriced on average.

It is common in most models of IPO pricing to ignore the roles of market participants not directly concerned in the informational asymmetry being assumed. Hence principal-agent models "ignore" investor behavior, adverse selection models "ignore" the distinction between issuer and underwriter, etc. For reasons that will become apparent later, this modeling approach is necessary if the resulting analysis is to be tractable. In truth, of course, issuers, investment bankers, distribution syndicates, and investors of various stripes and ability all undoubtedly have their roles to play. A synthesis of all these factors into a single theory awaits an analytic superman (or superwoman).

While underpricing is certainly the most modeled aspect of IPOs, IPOs present a rich list of additional phenomena which require elaboration. Although these additional issues have received far less attention than the underpricing paradox, some interesting theoretical work is available. Among the most prominent of these additional topics are the choice of offering type (i.e., firm commitment vs. best effort) and the explanation of "hot issues" markets, in which the volume of IPOs (and initial returns) rise substantially. Although our discussion in this chapter will emphasize theories of underpricing, we will briefly address these other models as well.

The chapter is organized as follows. First, we examine the adverse selection, principal agent, and signalling theories of IPO underpricing. Next we briefly examine a set of "heterodox," alternative theories of underpricing. Finally, we address some of the models designed to explain other aspects of IPO behavior.

ADVERSE SELECTION: THE ROCK MODEL AND VARIANTS

Perhaps the best known and most studied explanation of IPO underpricing is the adverse selection mechanism first formally proposed by Rock (1986), and analyzed by Beatty and Ritter (1986), Carter and Manaster (1990), Koh and Walter (1989), Ritter (1984), McStay (1992), and others.

Unlike many earlier explanations of IPO underpricing, the Rock mechanism provides a theoretically coherent model rich in structure and predictions. Underpricing is viewed as a consequence of rational behavior by issuing firms in an environment characterized by important informational asymmetries among potential investors. In particular, investors are differentiated by their levels of information about the true value of the issue, with "informed investors" (II's) having perfect (or superior) information, and "uninformed investors" (UI's) knowing only the probability distribution from which this value is drawn.[31] As a consequence of this asymmetry, II's compete with UI's only for "good" issues, creating an adverse selection mechanism in which UI's obtain shares in "bad" issues with greater probability. Hence, uninformed traders receive disproportionate levels of overpriced stocks. In order to induce UI's to participate in the IPO market, issuers must "leave some money on the table" by underpricing as compensation for the uninformed.

Although the adverse selection mechanism is easily described, Rock's analysis raises many interesting issues that will recur in our later evaluation of other underpricing models. Hence, we turn next to a detailed evaluation of Rock's insight.

Rock's model focuses on three types of agents: an issuing firm, II's, and UI's. The information structure implies, contrary to normal assumptions, that the issuing firm is not an "insider" as usually envisioned: the issuer knows no more about the value of the offering than do uninformed buyers. While this may seem unrealistic, the rationale for such an assumption is often given as disclosure requirements legally imposed on public offerings. By disclosing the financial condition of the firm, the proposed uses of the proceeds and the like, the firm has "shared" much of its relevant knowledge with the public. Thus, "uninformed" in this context is merely taken to mean "having less knowledge than II's."

Underwriters and investment bankers play no role in Rock (1986), although later analyses based on Rock's idea have focused on this complication. There are several functions underwriters might perform. First, in a firm commitment offering, underwriter purchase of a block of shares provides insurance to the issuing firm. This is relevant insofar as the offering is made to effect a diversification of insiders' portfolios. Second, underwriters may have information useful in valuing the offering, and indeed principal-agent analyses such as that of Baron (1982) highlight this aspect. Third, certain selective methods of rationing shares in oversubscribed offerings, a traditional function of the underwriters, may exacerbate or mitigate the degree of adverse selection, thereby increasing or reducing the level of underpricing required to induce UI's to participate.[32] Fourth, reputable underwriters may have the ability to "certify" the value of the issue, assuring uninformed potential buyers of its value and reducing or eliminating underpricing. Finally, underwriters may produce useful information on issue value through presale "solicitations of interest" aimed at knowledgeable investors, or by other means. We ignore these complications now but take them up again below.

Rock envisions an enterprise obligated to making a firm commitment offering of shares to the public. Because the firm has information on share value not superior to the UI's, the firm's behavior doesn't tell investors anything. Analysis is restricted to a single, one shot offering: later sales of equity and/or debt are ruled out. The firm and all potential investors know each others' financial circumstances, preferences, numbers, and, by inference, behavior.

Let z denote the number of shares offered and p the price per share. Let V be true value per share (revealed instantly in the aftermarket), where V is a random variable with known cumulative distribution $F(V)$ and mean value $E(V)$. Informed investors know V; the firm and the uninformed do not. Informed investors spend $\$I > 0$ on shares if $p < V$, but have zero demand if the issue is overpriced ($p > V$). Uninformed investors, of whom there are N, each invest a fraction T^* of their wealth in the issue. Each uninformed investor has wealth equal to 1, and any wealth not invested in IPO shares is put in a riskless, zero return security. Hence, this model is one of partial equilibrium in which other financial markets play no real role. Total dollar demands for IPO shares are thus:

(a) NT* + $I   if p < V
(b) NT*   if p > V   (1)

When shares are underpriced, orders by informed investors compete with those of UI's; yet when shares are too expensive, the uninformed are the only bidders. Rationing occurs when orders exceed the supply of shares. From the investor's point of view, the relevant issue is the difference in probabilities of receiving shares when shares are good versus when they are bad. How the rationing scheme works is critical. If ordering shares is costless, informed investors will order shares of any good offering (p < V) no matter how low the probability of an allocation. The UI's, however, cannot distinguish good offerings from bad. Hence, they will be concerned about the relative probabilities of receiving allocations of good versus bad shares. These probabilities in turn depend on the rationing rule. Rock assumes shares are rationed in purely random fashion, total orders being filled by lottery, so the resulting allocations show no favoritism between II's and UI's. Such a scheme implies that the probability a UI gets shares in a good offering, denoted b, is less than the probability b' of getting shares in a bad offering: b < b'. This immediately illustrates that pricing shares at their expected value E(V) will eliminate uninformed investors from the market, as they would be more likely to get bad shares, producing losses on average.

The above reasoning shows that participation by uninformed investors must require underpricing. This conclusion, though, is itself insufficient to explain why underpricing actually occurs. First, reducing prices may not work in attracting uninformed investors since, as offer proceeds fall, the informed demand $I can soak up a larger portion of the offering. This increases the adverse selection, dissuading UI's from placing orders. Second, it must be argued that price decreases have their expected effect of stimulating uninformed demand. This is important because one must explain why participation by uninformed investors is valuable to the issuer.

Since the issuer must underprice to attract orders from UI's, UI participation must be necessary or valuable to induce the issuer to seek it. Finally, it is not obvious that the model has an equilibrium such that the actions of investors (in particular, UI's), <u>conditioned on</u> their beliefs about the values of b and b', lead to optimizing behavior (T*) that in turn <u>determines</u> probabilities b and b' such that the UI's beliefs were correct in the first instance ("rational expectations").

To solve the problems mentioned above, Rock first analyzes the wealth allocation (investment) decision of an uninformed investor. Given that such an investor believes the probabilities of receiving allocations are b_e in the good state (V > p) and b_e' in the bad state (V < p), the investor's end of period expected utility is:

$$EU = b_e(1 - F(p)) \, E[U(1 + T(p^{-1}V - 1)) \,|\, V > p]$$

$$+ \, b_e'F(p)E[U(1 + T(p^{-1}V - 1)) \,|\, V \leq p] \tag{2}$$

$$+ \, [1 - b_e \, (1 - F(p)) - b_e'F(p)]U(1)$$

where E denotes expectations, U is the utility function, F ($\cdot$) is the cumulative distribution function of share values, and all wealth is invested in the riskless asset if no allocation is received. The UI selects a percentage T of the wealth to try to invest in IPO shares to maximize the expected utility. The optimal choice T* will then depend on b_e, b_e', and p, and we write $T^* = T^* \, (b_e, b_e', p)$. One can show, in fact, that T* depends not on b_e and b_e' individually, but only on their ratio (b_e/b_e'), and we might refer to this ratio as the rationing <u>bias</u> resulting from adverse selection with the filling of orders by lottery.

Next, Rock establishes the existence of an equilibrium with the following rational expectations property. Suppose that beliefs b_e and b_e' induce UI's to invest a fraction of their wealth T in the

IPO. This in turn determines the allocation probability b by the relationship:

$$b = \min ((pz/(NT^* + I)), 1) \qquad (3)$$

Rock shows that $b = b_e$ for some b_e, so that there is a rational expectations equilibrium whenever $p < E(V)$.

Demonstrating that the level of uniformed demand increases as price decreases is somewhat more difficult, and here Rock relies on a "large market" assumption to simplify analysis. When there are many uninformed investors, investment in the IPO represents only a small fraction of their wealth. Yet, if each investor has a smooth (differentiable) utility function, then each is approximately risk neutral with respect to such a small gamble. Hence, zero expected profits to uninformed investors determine their chances of getting good shares when bad shares are not rationed. This fact is useful in demonstrating that, as price is lowered, the probability of obtaining good shares b does not fall so rapidly that, despite the price decrease, uninformed demand declines.

Having established the existence of a rational expectations equilibrium and downward sloping uninformed demand curve, one can turn to two basic questions. First, under what conditions would the owners be willing to underprice? Second, if underpricing is optimal, what is the optimal discount (degree of underpricing)?

A variety of circumstances can motivate the owners to go public by underpricing, although the most obvious motive, risk aversion and diversification, is perhaps the must plausible assumption. Since the demand of the uninformed is downward sloping in price, price decreases trade offering proceeds for greater certainty in selling out the offering even if it is bad.[33] Thus, sufficiently risk averse owners can be expected to pursue such a policy in the absence of other, more attractive opportunities. An example of this sort is constructed by Rock (1986), while McStay (1992) offers a useful discussion of the circumstances under which a closely held firm would elect to go public in an underpricing equilibrium.

Determination of the optimal offer price in Rock type models is analytically difficult due to the complex nature of uninformed demand and the binary nature of informed demand. Rock (1986) and McStay (1992) offer numerical examples. It is important to note, however, that risk aversion on the part of the owners is not, by itself, a useful explanation of underpricing since such an argument could not explain the serious underpricing observed in best efforts offerings. (See Tinic (1988) for a modern statement, and Bear and Curley (1975) for an earlier point of view.)

As mentioned above, Rock's analysis utilizes a number of simplifying assumptions, and subsequent elaboration on Rock's idea has focused primarily on weakening these assumptions and analyzing the model for its comparative static properties. Empirical tests have also been conducted and will be reviewed in the next chapter.

Among the most important extensions of Rock's work are: (1) Beatty and Ritter's analysis of the roles of share value uncertainty and underwriter certification in underpricing; (2) Carter and Manaster's study of information gathering and underwriter reputation; and (3) Koh and Walter's direct test of Rock's equilibrium condition of normal returns to UI's.

Beatty and Ritter (1986) argue that there is a positive relationship between the degree of uncertainty over share value (given by characteristics of the distribution of values $F(V)$) and the extent of underpricing. In particular, as share values become more uncertain (more widely dispersed), the differing probabilities of getting good versus bad shares become more important since bad shares become even worse.[34] This share value uncertainty is termed "ex ante uncertainty" to distinguish it from the more familiar systematic risk measured by Beta coefficients. Thus, adverse selection is a more serious problem for more highly speculative offerings. Given that offerings vary in their dispersions of values, however, why do owners of speculative firms underprice more when such a risky status might be initially concealed? Beatty and Ritter suggest that underwriters play a role in enforcing an equilibrium in which firms with highly uncertain values underprice more. The reputations of investment bankers are viewed as valuable assets which the underwriters wish to conserve and protect. Faced with a more speculative offering, underwriters select lower offering prices in order to avoid later punishment by either investors (if they underprice too little) or issuing firms (if they underprice too much). Hence, one expects investment bankers who deviate from expected behavior to lose market share, a proposition for which Beatty and Ritter offer some empirical support.

Carter and Manaster (1990) also emphasize the role of investment banker reputation, but additionally focus on information acquisition activities by investors. They argue that highly uncertain offerings trigger increases in information gathering efforts.[35] This in turn increases the percentages of informed investors, worsening the adverse selection bias against uninformed investors. So long as such UIs are still needed, the degree of underpricing must be greater. Since underpricing is not desirable to issuing firms, one would expect highly speculative firms to attempt to masquerade as low risk issuers. Here, however, investment bankers have a role to play. In particular, a desire to protect their reputation induces prestigious underwriters to select only less speculative offerings. Hence, lower risk firms can try to signal their high quality by selecting prestigious underwriters who underprice less than their less prestigious competitors, and underwriter prestige should be a credible guarantee of limited informed trading. Carter and Manaster offer some empirical support for these claims.[36]

As previous discussion makes clear, a critical feature of Rock's model is the assumed "democratic" method of rationing shares when an offer is oversubscribed. In the U.S. it is frequently alleged that preferred or regular customers of distributing brokers are given preferential treatment in share allotments, and U.S. law allows greater latitude than do the regulations of many other countries. If underwriters allotted oversubscribed shares so that uninformed investors had better chances of obtaining allocations, adverse selection and underpricing would presumably be reduced. This idea has been used as the basis of several empirical tests of the Rock adverse selection mechanism, including those of Koh and Walter (1989) and McStay (1992), discussed in the next chapter.

PRINCIPAL-AGENT: BARON'S MORAL HAZARD MODEL OF UNDERPRICING

In the previous section we saw how Kevin Rock developed a theoretically consistent model of underpricing based on two primary assumptions: potential investors are differentially informed about the value of the issue, and the issuing firm/underwriter does not have useful private information on the issuing firm's prospects. While it is almost certainly true that some investors know more about an issue than others, much informal criticism of Rock's approach stems from the assumption that the issuing firm knows no more than do "uninformed" investors. Indeed, it is precisely the idea that firm "insiders" -- original owners and managers -- know more than others that led to the wholesale application of strategic/game theoretic reasoning and information economics to financial analysis.

Since Ross's (1973) pioneering paper, utilization of the "principal-agent" framework to analyze financial decision making has become widespread. In analyses of this kind, one imagines that an economic actor, called the "principal," hires an "agent" to transact some business for him. The principal offers the agent a contract which specifies the agent's rewards, depending on some observable features of the outcome of the agent's actions. For example, sales representatives receive commissions based on their sales outcome. Typically, the basis for remuneration depends not just on the agent's efforts, but also on some random factors unobserved by one or both parties. The principal, who has all the bargaining power, cannot perfectly monitor the agent's behavior. Further, the agent may have important information unavailable to the principal. The principal's problem, then, is to construct a contract that: (1) is at least minimally acceptable to the agent, (2) induces the agent to behave in the principal's interest, and (3) induces the agent to reveal or make appropriate use of any private information the agent might possess. Any such contract also will determine how risks are shared between the principal and agent. Such models are common in economics and financial research.

Baron (1982) applies principal-agent analysis to the IPO underpricing paradox. Unlike Rock's model, Baron assumes that the investment banker/underwriter has information superior to that of the firm. This information may represent intimate knowledge of market conditions, investor contacts, or industry trends relevant to the issuer's financial prospects. The model is "one shot" with no role for dynamic competition among underwriters, nor for reputation building. Analysis focuses on the optimal behavior of the issuing firm (the principal) and the investment banker (the agent) hired to execute the offering. Underwriting, which has an insurance benefit for the issuer, is ignored by assuming risk neutrality of both major participants.

The principal can choose from among three types of contracts. First, the investment bank can be used to distribute shares only, a "distribution contract." Second, the banker can be entirely bypassed with the principal selling shares directly to the public. Finally, the issuer can use a "delegation contract" in which the investment bank (indirectly) prices the offering and undertakes efforts to stimulate demand. Because Baron's principal-agent model is quite complex, our discussion will focus primarily on its underlying intuition. Readers interested in technical details can see Baron (1982) and the principal-agent survey of Rees (1987).

Proceeds from the sale of shares x depend on share price p, investment bank effort (promotion) e, and market conditions θ.

Market conditions are unknown at the time the contract is formulated; yet, the agent (banker) sees an informative signal δ that affects the distribution of θ. Thus, the probability distribution $g(x \mid p,e,\delta)$ summarizes the distribution of proceeds x given p,e, and δ. Further, $x(p,e,\theta)$ is increasing in effort e, and increases in effort yield increases in proceeds in the sense of first degree stochastic dominance.[37]

Let d be the bank's claim (which may be untruthful) about its market information δ. The compensation to the investment bank is s(p,d,x). Hence, the bank first learns about market conditions δ, and reports a value d to the issuer (principal). If the issuer proceeds with the offer, it selects a price p(d) based on the bank's "advice" d. The bank privately selects its level of promotion activity e to serve its interests. Payment to the bank is then s(p,d,x), and returns to the issuer are just (x - s).

The bank acts in its own interests given the contract offered by the issuer. Since promotion is costly, write the bank's returns as s - c(e) where c(e) is the cost associated with a promotion level e. The bank, therefore, selects its effort e and reports on market conditions d to maximize its expected returns given: (1) its information δ, (2) the pricing rule p(d) selected by the issuer, (3) its costs c(e), and (4) the compensation contract (formula) s(p(d), d, x) = s(d, x) selected by the issuer/principal. The issuing firm knows all this and takes account of it in making its plans.

At this point it is necessary to explain a few technical issues that arise in principal-agent models. First, the principal will be selecting a contract to maximize expected proceeds. Such a contract is a function of or a relationship between values of d and x and levels of agent compensation. This sort of optimization problem is much more complex than merely selecting values for a few control variables. It often requires solution by specialized techniques such as the calculus of variations or optimal control. Interest usually focuses on qualitative features of the contract; for example, "does compensation increase when proceeds x increase?" Analysis can be quite difficult.

Because of the inherent mathematical complexity of principal-agent models, derivation of an optimal contract is often simplified by using the so-called "revelation principle," a mathematical device that facilitates analysis. As an example, suppose a government (principal) collects income taxes from citizens. The citizens report their incomes and are taxed accordingly. Suppose the government decides that taxes should be higher for those making $100,000 than for those making $80,000. Further, imagine that the government cannot tell the difference between people making $80,000 and $100,000 (although all other incomes can be observed), and solely relies on citizens' reports. If citizens are purely self-interested, all those making $100,000 will claim they make $80,000, yielding tax receipts at the $80,000 rate. The revelation principle notes that, in any such situation, there is another tax system that yields the same tax revenues but induces everyone to tell the truth about their income. In this case, the government need only tax $80,000 and $100,000 incomes at the same level (in dollars). Then the same revenue would be raised, and those making $100,000 would have no reason to lie about it.

The revelation principle is important because it allows the analyst to restrict attention to contracts that induce the agent to tell the truth. Any lying is taken into account and made unnecessary by the design of the contract. This principle says nothing substantive about how contracts look, but merely simplifies their analysis.

Technical complications aside, we proceed to analyze the principal's problem. The principal tries to design a contract $s(\delta,x)$ that specifies agent compensation based on any private information δ and proceeds x and a pricing rule $p(\delta)$ that establishes price per share based on the agent's (truthful) report δ in order to maximize expected proceeds from the offering. Formally, the problem has the form:

$$\max_{p(\delta),s(\delta,x)} \quad \int \left(\int (x-s)g(x \mid p(\delta), e(\delta,\delta),\delta)dx \right)f(\delta)d\delta \qquad (4)$$

s.t.

(i) $s(\delta,x) - c(e(\delta,\delta)) \geq s(d,x) - c(e(d,\delta))$
(ii) $e(d,\delta)$ maximizes the agent's returns
(iii) expected agent returns exceed a minimum level

Expression (4) indicates that the issuer is to select a pricing rule $p(\delta)$ and contract $s(\delta,x)$ to maximize expected returns $(x-s)$ from the offering.[38] The constraints represent the requirements of truthful revelation of δ by the agent and agent rationality. Constraint (i) implies that if δ is the true signal, then claiming that the signal is δ must be at least as good for the agent as claiming that it is d not equal to δ, no matter what δ is. The term $e(d,\delta)$ is defined in constraint (ii): $e(d,\delta)$ is that level of effort that most benefits the agent, given the contract s and pricing rule p, when δ is the true market signal and d is reported to the principal. Constraint (iii) is a participation condition: the agent must expect at least some minimal returns to be willing to participate in the contract. Hence, the constraints collectively indicate that: (1) the agent will be given an incentive to tell the truth; (2) the agent will be self-beneficial, and (3) the agent is willing to work for the principal only when at least some minimum returns are expected to be received.

Several conclusions can be obtained from analysis of the problem in expression (4). First, since e and δ are not directly observed by the principal, the agent's choice of effort will not equal that level of effort which maximizes total net benefits, i.e., moral hazard will arise.[39] Even though the issuer knows this, it is typically too costly to give the agent incentives to work maximally. Inducing the agent to work harder (increase e) typically requires that the principal award the agent a larger share of the proceeds, a costly procedure. Additionally, truthful revelation by the agent usually requires costly distortions in the contract. Thus, one does not expect that the agent will behave in a manner that maximizes total net benefits (proceeds minus effort costs).

Because of the great complexity of the model, Baron considers contracts having the special form $S(\delta,x) = S(\delta) + tX$, where t, $0 \leq t \leq 1$, is the share of the proceeds given to the banker. With this simplification a number of conclusions are possible. Note that $t=1$ represents a firm commitment contract in which the investment banker receives all proceeds after a fixed payment to the issuer, while $t = 0$ approximately corresponds to a pure best efforts offering. Baron shows that with effort fixed at the "first best" level (that level that maximizes total net benefits given δ), the optimal price $p(\delta)$ is lower than the net benefit maximizing optimal price. This suggests that the model may explain underpricing.

Baron continues by analyzing an example utilizing relatively simple forms for the cost, utility, and proceeds functions, and a uniformly distributed market signal δ. These simplifications allow several interesting propositions to be derived. The level of uncertainty the issuer faces with respect to the banker's information, given by the dispersion of the distribution of δ, is positively related to the willingness of the issuer to accept a lower price. Hence, uncertainty in this sense is positively related to underpricing. This conclusion, while derived under special assumptions, is quite generally plausible and is common to several types of IPO underpricing models. Further, this notion that greater uncertainty induces greater underpricing was expressed in very early analyses of IPO underpricing which did not utilize theoretical models.

Baron's general conclusions are as follows. First, if the issuer and banker had the same information on the state of the capital market, then a pure firm commitment contract would always be optimal. This occurs because by selling all the shares to the bank, the bank gains an incentive to promote the issue optimally: the bank will select its selling efforts to maximize the total net proceeds of the offering. The issuer receives a fixed payment in this case. If, however, the bank has superior information, then a distribution contract is likely to produce moral hazard: the bank won't work hard enough. In this case the issuer may improve the returns by "delegating" pricing to the bank, i.e., by utilizing information from the bank to price the issue. The bank will earn a return for its special information. The example illustrates that this may result in underpricing. This conclusion can arise because by underpricing the shares, the issuer reduces the costs of assuring truthful advice from the banker.

Baron's model establishes that underpricing could arise because of a principal-agent relationship between the issuer and investment banker. It is important to recognize, however, the limitations of this analysis. First, the complexity of the model makes interpretation of some of the results difficult. Underpricing can occur, but such a result probably depends on some technical assumptions that are difficult to verify in practice. Second, principal-agent models implicitly rely on strong market structure assumptions. Would not competition among investment bankers mitigate the moral hazard problems in an environment with reputation building? Finally, the information asymmetry used by Baron may not be a realistic description of many IPOs.

Underpricing can arise in Baron's model only when the investment banker has information superior to the issuer. If both had symmetric information, a firm commitment offering with no advising would arise in which underpricing would not occur and moral hazard would be absent. This fact allows for the clever test of Baron's model presented by Muscarella and Vetsuypens (1989), who examine initial excess return behavior in IPOs of shares in the investment banks themselves. In these "self marketed IPOs," an investment bank "goes public" and promotes/distributes its own shares. Since here the principal and agent are the same firm, no information asymmetry should arise. Yet, Muscarella and

Vetsuypens find underpricing in these issues, a result not supportive of Baron's explanation.

SIGNALLING MODELS OF UNDERPRICING

Unlike the assumptions made about informed/uniformed
investors by adverse selection models, and the knowledgeable
underwriter framework utilized in principal-agent theories of
underpricing, signalling models posit that the issuing firm knows
more about its prospects than do any other market participants.
This specification is attractive because it coincides quite closely
with an important area of modern finance theory: firm insiders
know more than outsiders, leading to interesting strategic aspects
in firm announcement, dividend, production, and investment
behavior.[40] A vast literature has arisen which analyzes precisely
this sort of informational asymmetry.

Although the idea of signalling behavior has seen wide
application in financial analysis, the notion of signalling was first
introduced by Spence (1973) in his analysis of the role of education
in labor market behavior. Spence questioned whether a worker's
educational attainment should be legitimately rewarded by an
employer even if the education was, in itself, totally "worthless" as
far as job performance was concerned? Could not educational
credentials themselves convey valuable information on the
unobserved quality of the worker? Since virtually all workers can
be expected to claim they are of high quality, mere assertions are
unconvincing. Yet, high quality workers, if they know they are of
high quality, have an incentive to try to prove this fact to employers, just as low quality workers may desire to masquerade as high
quality employees. Is there any action high quality workers could
take that would convince potential employers of their quality?
Signalling models are concerned with this basic and widely
applicable issue.

The canonical signalling problem is as follows. Market participants are assumed to differ in some unobservable but important way. Transactions among participants can produce increased welfare or other benefits. Participants with "good" characteristics would benefit if they could somehow convince other participants of their quality. Hence, such actors seek forms of behavior, called signals, that provide convincing proof of their value. Since participants with low quality characteristics could enjoy greater benefits if others incorrectly believed them to be high quality participants, any behavior successfully used as a signal must be more costly to poor quality players to dissuade their charade. In Spence's education signalling model, it was assumed that good workers could obtain education at lower costs than poor workers. Although good workers are more valuable to employers and can command higher wages, bad workers are dissuaded from obtaining education because it is so costly for them that the wage gains of being taken for a good worker are insufficiently attractive. Spence showed that an equilibrium was possible in which good workers got education, bad workers did not, and educated workers received higher wages. Such an equilibrium is called "separating" because the unobserved "types" (characteristics) of participants are revealed by their actions. If, however, education costs differed little among workers, low quality workers might obtain education in order to appear to be good quality, destroying the value of the signal. In cases like this, workers' types are not credibly distinguished by their behavior, leading to a so-called "pooling" equilibrium in which all workers behave the same and are treated the same by employers.[41]

An important feature of signalling models is that the behavior that constitutes the signal occurs prior to offers being made for transactions. Hence, the informed participants move first. In contrast, "screening" models assume that the informed players act after, and in response to, offers made by the uninformed player(s). This distinction is quite important for the possible existence of separating and pooling type equilibria. For institutional reasons that will become apparent below, underpricing models have uniformly adopted the signalling framework.

Application of the signalling mechanism to modelling an IPO relies on the idea that firms are differentiated by their values, and that these values, while unobserved by potential investors, are nevertheless known by the firms themselves. High value firms would obviously like to convince investors of their good quality in order to realize greater proceeds from the sales of their securities. Yet, mere claims of high quality may be unconvincing. Hence, the firms need to find some action that is: (1) not too costly, and (2) unlikely to be imitated by low value firms seeking to mislead potential investors.

In a pathbreaking application of the signalling idea to financial theory, Leland and Pyle (1977) argue that the level of retention of shares by the original owners can be a convincing signal of firm value to outsiders. Since the inside owners are presumably risk averse, and since their ownership in the firm may represent a large, undiversified risk, retaining some percentage of the shares (perhaps for later sale in a seasoned offering) is less costly for owners of high value firms than for owners of low value firms. If firm value may be (will be) revealed later, holding a large fraction of shares could make sense only for high value firm owners. In fact, the percentage of shares retained is fully informative in their model, allowing investors to perfectly calculate firm value V via the CAPM derived relationship:

$$V = (- b \, z \, / \, (1 + r)) \, [\alpha + \ln (1 - \alpha)] + K \qquad (5)$$

where V is firm value, r is the risk free interest rate, b is the coefficient of risk aversion in the entrepreneur's mean-variance utility function, K is capital outlay for the project,

$Z = (\sigma_X^2 \sigma_M^2 - [COV(\overline{x}, \overline{M})]^2) / \sigma_M^2$ represents the specific risk of the project (equal to the variance of project returns $\sigma_X{}^2$ if such returns are uncorrelated with market returns), $\sigma_M{}^2$ is the variance of market returns, COV indicates the covariance between IPO returns $\overline{x}$ and market returns $\overline{M}$, and α is the fraction of equity retained by the entrepreneur.

Leland and Pyles' results, while quite important, do not provide a theory of IPO underpricing. Since entrepreneur share retention is fully revealing, underpricing of shares need never occur. By observing α and inferring the relationship in equation (5), investors know exactly what firm value is; so there is no purpose in underpricing shares. Further, the Leland-Pyle signalling equilibrium is not automatic and requires additional conditions (e.g., fewness of high value firms) to exist.

As is so often the case, Leland and Pyles' insight leads to more or less contemporaneous application of the signalling mechanism by several authors. The papers of Allen and Faulhaber (1989), Grinblatt and Hwang (1989), and Welch (1989) are especially notable: all seek to explain underpricing via signalling behaviors that are at least moderately similar to that described by Leland and Pyle (1977). Before we examine the logic underlying these contributions, several important points must be made.

First, one requirement for an action to be a signal is that it is observable. "Underpricing," per se, would appear to fail this test since it is not immediately clear that underpricing is always recognized as such. To be underpriced, a stock must have a known, "correct" price below which it is being sold. Yet, the "correct" price is presumably the information a high value firm would wish to signal. In any event, if pricing is to be a signal of value, one must explain how that signal can be recognized and interpreted by potential investors.

The argument above is not in itself really damning of signalling explanations of underpricing. First, it may in fact be possible for investors to recognize underpricing when they see it.

Second, underpricing may occur merely to facilitate some other form of signalling, such as the share retention procedure of Leland and Pyle, high dividends, retention of prestigious (i.e., expensive) financial advisors, and the like. The second explanation suggests that underpricing could be merely a consequence of some signalling equilibrium and not an activity pursued for its own sake. How various signalling models deal with this issue probably constitutes an important distinction between them.

We note also that for any signalling model to make sense, there must be some gains for high value issuers in signalling their values. To explain initial underpricing, the owners clearly must retain some shares which they plan to sell (at the high prices resulting from their signalling) in a later, seasoned offering. To put it bluntly, shares are underpriced now to prove they are good so that later offerings command higher proceeds.

A final caveat must be applied to signalling explanations of underpricing. If a firm wishes to signal its value, it is not necessarily the case that underpricing is the best way. Given the enormous number of issuable claims, legal arrangements and other types of observable behavior open to firms, underpricing may be a feasible but overly expensive way to signal. The attractiveness of underpricing as a signal must depend on its immediate character. Unlike "burning money" activities firms might use to signal, underpricing directly benefits investors and thus need not be monitored. Additionally, investor lawsuit risks may be reduced by underpricing (Tinic (1988)).

The signalling models of Allen and Faulhaber (1989), Grinblatt and Hwang (1989), Welch (1989), Nanda (1988), and others differ in some respects, and none seems inherently superior. Since the analysis of Grinblatt and Hwang is closest in form and notation to that of Leland and Pyle (1977), we select it for more extensive discussion.[42]

Grinblatt and Hwang (hereafter GH) posit a three period world in which an entrepreneur owns some investment project requiring a given, fixed investment at date 0 of \$K to pursue.[43] The project yields cash flows in dates 1 and 2. Date 2 cash flow is $\mu + X_2$, where X_2 is some random variable with zero mean and variance $\sigma^2 > 0$, and μ is fixed and known to the entrepreneur. At date 1 a random, independent (i.e., uninformative) cash flow of X_1 arises with zero mean and variance σ^2.[44] The entrepreneur is risk averse and, to diversify, wishes to market the project to the risk neutral public in an IPO. The entrepreneur (hereafter issuer) knows μ and σ^2, while investors only know the distribution from which these values are drawn. If μ is "high," the issuer would like to prove this to investors. Unfortunately, the Leland and Pyle signal of the fraction of shares retained, denoted α, is not by itself a good signal of μ since investors do not know σ^2. A large α, for example, might indicate high μ and large σ^2, or lower μ and smaller variance. The larger the variance σ^2, the greater is the cost of retaining shares to the risk averse issuer. Thus, the issuer would desire to inform investors when σ^2 is high in order to make the α signal informative and effective. Since two items of information need to be signaled, two signals are needed. Offer price p constitutes the other signal.

Without signalling, investors learn μ for free with probability θ, $0 < \theta < 1$, between dates 0 and 1. Otherwise, μ is revealed at date 2. The order of events is as follows. First, luck selects μ and σ^2, and the issuer sees them. Then, the issuer offers a fraction $1-\alpha$ of the firm to outsiders at price p at date 0. Investors accept or reject the offer. Then, investors learn μ with probability θ and learn nothing with probability $1-\theta$. Date 1 arrives, and the issuer disposes of the remaining shares at the date 1 market price after the public realization of date 1 cash flow X_1. Date 2 then occurs, μ is revealed, and payoffs to investors are made. It is assumed everyone knows all this.

Since the issuer sells out at date 1, the selections of α and p are intended to maximize the expected utility U of date 1 wealth W_1, which takes the simple quadratic form:

$$E (U (W_1)) = E (W_1) - (b/2) \sigma^2 (W_1) \qquad (6)$$

Here, b represents the issuer's risk aversion and $\sigma^2 (W_1)$ the variance of the date 1 wealth. The issuer allocates initial wealth between shares retained in the IPO, a risk free asset, and a market fund, priced via the CAPM relationship. For simplicity, project returns are uncorrelated with the market.[45]

Let $E (\mu|\alpha, p)$ be the investor's guess about μ given the signals α and p. (Investors are risk neutral; so they don't care about σ^2 except to the extent it allows them to interpret the signal α.) Investors initially buy $(1 - \alpha)$ of the shares if $p < E (\mu|\alpha, p)$ and nothing otherwise. At period 1 the aftermarket exhibits price $p_1 = E (\mu|\alpha, p)$ if μ is not revealed, and $p_1 = \mu$ if it is.

If σ^2 were known, the GH model would closely resemble Leland and Pyle (1977), producing similar conclusions. When σ^2 is not known, however, p can be used to signal this value. It becomes clear that this is possible only when it is recognized that there is a one-to-one correspondence between the signalling model in which investors use α and p to infer μ and σ^2, and a signalling model in which they use α and the underpricing discount D to infer μ and σ^2. Given this correspondence, GH demonstrate that a signalling equilibrium exists that is fully separating: the signals α and p allow investors to infer μ and σ^2 for any firm. The signalling schedules used by investors and firms in equilibrium are:

(i) $\qquad \mu = \mu^L (\alpha) + [(1 - \alpha) / (1 - \alpha r)] D \qquad (7)$

(ii) $\qquad \sigma^2 = \sigma_L^2 + [(1 - \alpha) r / (1 - \alpha r) \alpha b] D$

where D is the discount, $\mu^L (\alpha) = (- r^{-2}) b \sigma_L^2 [\ln (1 - r) + r] + K$, and σ_L^2 is the lowest project return variance among potential issuers. An equivalent statement in terms of α and p is available as well.

While derivation of equilibrium in the GH signalling model is technically complex, the equilibrium itself has a number of intuitive and appealing properties. First, it is straightforward to show that high variance projects are sold at larger discounts in equilibrium, a result consistent with empirical evidence and other, competing theories. Further, given any variance of returns σ^2, issuers with high value projects retain a greater fraction of shares α. Additionally, given σ^2, underpricing is greater for higher value projects.

The GH signalling equilibrium works for the following reasons. When the project is valuable, the issuer wishes to demonstrate this. By issuing at a lower initial price, the issuer "proves" that the variance of the project is higher, which in turn "proves" that the issuer's fractional holding α is especially costly. Since the issuer is risk averse, retaining more shares is unpleasant. Discounting the price is costly but is necessary to demonstrate the worth of the signal α. Hence, underpricing arises as a way of establishing the reliability of the other, more conventional signal, and is of no further independent significance. It is necessary to point out that for most signalling models there exist several equilibria, only some of which may be separating. Pooling equilibria, in which firms types cannot be distinguished by their actions, are also possible. Typically, the sort of equilibrium one expects to obtain may depend on various technical assumptions about parameter values in the model, and often criteria used to eliminate "bad" equilibria are insufficiently strong to produce a unique equilibrium. This would appear to be a defect in signalling explanations of underpricing, since all that one is usually able to show is that there are equilibria involving signalling and that these equilibria "may occur." This supposed disadvantage may in some ways be an advantage. Empirical evidence suggests that the levels and frequency of underpricing vary significantly through time (Ibbotson and Jaffe (1975), Ritter (1984)). Periods of very high initial excess returns have been dubbed "Hot Issues" markets, and

Allen and Faulhaber (1989) argue that exogenously driven changes in investment opportunities could cause changes in the sorts of equilibria one sees through time. "Hot Issues" markets are separating equilibria in which underpricing is widely employed as a signal. When market opportunities change, pooling equilibria involving no underpricing emerge. While such arguments are admittedly informal, signalling models, with their multiplicity of equilibria, may be more successful at explaining the secular behavior of initial returns through time than are competing models such as Rock (1986), which must rely on particular changes in the compositions of initial offerings. No real dynamic theory of "Hot Issues" markets has yet been proposed.

HETERODOX EXPLANATIONS OF UNDERPRICING

Although the adverse selection, principal-agent/moral hazard, and signalling models of IPO behavior constitute the most widely discussed explanations of underpricing, a number of alternative theories have been proposed in the literature. Some of these alternative formulations -- particularly the older ones -- have not been formally developed to completion, although several others are theoretically coherent and must be seriously considered as at least partial alternative explanations for this puzzling phenomenon.

Competing heterodox theories of underpricing include: the lawsuit avoidance theory of Tinic (1988), the incomplete spanning arguments of Mauer and Senbet (1992), the presale information gathering model of Benveniste and Spindt (1989), the monopoly power argument, the "Cascades" theory of Welch (1992), the divergence of opinion argument of Miller (1977), and early views attributing underpricing to risk aversion of one sort or another. We briefly discuss these models below.

Tinic (1988) presents a simple theoretical model suggesting that underpricing may represent a form of insurance against lawsuits by disgruntled investors. The reputations of underwriters, which are temporally valuable assets, can be damaged by widely publicized legal troubles, and it would be surprising if investment banks did not take some precautions against this risk. Underpricing may reduce this risk since losses on shares then become less likely.[46]

Formally, Tinic views the underwriters' and issuers' expected liability costs at time t, denoted E [L_t], as equal to:

$$E [L_t] = f (P_t/P_0) \cdot g (P_0 - P_t) \qquad (8)$$

where f ( ) represents the probability of a settlement or judgment, P_t is the price at t, P_0 is the offer price, and g ($\cdot$) is the expected damages given a lawsuit. Arguing that post offer relative prices may follow a lognormal distribution through time, Tinic shows that an offer price below the "true value" P^* of the shares reduces expected liabilities at all future dates.

To support this theory, Tinic examines underpricing levels before and after the Securities Act of 1933. This act greatly expanded investor opportunities to pursue lawsuits against issuers and their underwriters. Tinic finds increased underpricing since the act, and notes that the current "multi-tiered" structure of the investment banking industry, in which prestigious firms restrict themselves to higher quality offerings, is a post-1933 phenomenon. The results on pre- and post-1933 underpricing are important in themselves since such evidence appears inconsistent with, for example, a pure asymmetric information theory such as Rock (1986).

Benveniste and Spindt (1989) offer a novel explanation of underpricing that emphasizes the role of market information acquisition by investment bankers through "presale solicitations of interest." Prior to choosing price for a new issue, investment banks form a "roadshow" and make presentations to potential investors, brokers, and others. Indications of interest (or lack of interest) expressed by these investors may be valuable market signals useful in pricing the issue. As in Rock (1986), investors are of two types, "occasional" (i.e., uninformed) and "regular" (or informed). Regular investors have valuable private signals on the worth of the issue. The difficulty, of course, is to provide investors who have favorable private information with an incentive to reveal it. Merely paying for good information triggers a flood of bogus "good" information. The incentive problem is solved, however, by giving preferential allocations of shares to regular investors with good news to share about the issuer's prospects. The system is maintained by blackballing regular investors whose participation is unsatisfactory. Hence, underpricing is a way of compensating regular investors for revealing their private information.[47]

The Benveniste and Spindt mechanism resembles a kind of auction and has several interesting empirical implications. First, when a bit of favorable news is relatively more valuable (i.e., leads to more favorable forecasts), underpricing levels rise. Extensive preselling should also be associated with greater underpricing. Finally, high interest in the offering should presage greater underpricing. Empirical support for some of these propositions appears in Beatty and Ritter (1986) and Welch (1989), though no formal test of this model has yet been undertaken.

A radically different (yet thoroughly conventional) explanation for underpricing is offered by Mauer and Senbet (1992). Unlike other theories that typically posit information asymmetries to explain discounts, Mauer and Senbet argue that incomplete spanning of IPO securities by the secondary market may explain underpricing. This means that no portfolio of securities tradeable on the secondary market is capable of replicating the returns of securities offered in IPOs. Adopting the common factors approach used to explain security prices in arbitrage pricing models, Mauer and Senbet suggest that underpricing in the primary market reflects a "primary market risk premium" that results from incomplete spanning. This occurs because access to the primary market is limited; so the primary and secondary markets can be viewed as segmented. Some portion of IPO security cash flows is unspanned by secondary market securities, generating a primary market risk premium that arises from the risk aversion of investors with access to the primary market, and the primary risk factor. Both limited access and incompletely spanned cash flows are needed to generate the result. The model implies that IPO underpricing should be unrelated to systematic risks as measured by beta (β) coefficients, increasing with IPO "residual risk" (the variance of the unspanned component in IPO cash flows), and systematically variable across industry classifications when such classifications imply differences in spanning and investor access. Further, as more IPOs occur in a given "new" industry, underpricing of later offerings should decline as spanning via previously floated securities increases. Mauer and Senbet offer some empirical support for these propositions although factors such as investor "access" are, admittedly, difficult to quantify.

Welch (1992) offers an interesting "dynamic" model of IPOs which alone among models of underpricing, recognizes the sequential nature of share sales. While virtually all previous models implicitly assume that investor purchases of shares occur at a single point in time, Welch argues that later potential investors may learn from observing the behavior of earlier ones. This idea is consistent with informal information about the initial marketing of some IPOs, and may offer an explanation of underpricing.[48]

In Welch's model, investors obtain private signals about the value or quality of the offered shares. Investors are approached and offered shares sequentially, with later investors being able to observe what earlier investors do. Yet the actions of early investors presumably reveal something about the information (signals) they possess. Buying by early investors may result in a later investor buying even when information is discouraging. Thus, the order in which investors are approached is important and can determine the success of the offering. When early selling activity results in later investors "ignoring" their private information, a chain reaction, termed a "cascade" by Welch, can ensue. These results are not dependent on the issuer having no inside information: issuers can receive private signals as well.

Welch's model explains underpricing even when the issuer is risk neutral. Because of the possibility of a cascade, issuers are induced to reduce initial prices. Further, issuers of good shares may price high enough that the offer can fail. Offers should succeed or fail quickly, and issuers may have an incentive to seek to limit investor-to-investor communication, or to perhaps bribe early potential investors.

The cascades model highlights the dynamic nature of investor behavior and produces appealing predictions. The success or failure of an offering need not be convincing evidence of its quality (or lack thereof). It does appear, however, that the cascades mechanism could depend on restrictions on, or imperfect flexibility of, investor share order sizes. Earlier investors are not typically faced with a take it or leave it situation, but can adjust the size of their orders as they see fit. Behavior of this sort may produce almost intractable problems in the analysis of cascade type sequential selling models. Further, the applicability of this mechanism clearly depends on general observability of (early) investor behavior.

Miller (1977), in a widely discussed paper, suggests that IPO "underpricing" actually reflects the effects of investor divergence of opinion and rationing in oversubscribed offerings. In simple terms, suppose that investors place a wide variety of values on IPO shares. If rationing occurs in their sale, then in general there is no guarantee that those investors who place the highest values on the shares obtain their desired holdings. Once secondary market trading begins, the shares are reallocated towards the highest evaluators, and competition for shares leads to the first day price increase.

This simple and intuitively appealing explanation of underpricing has not received general support for several reasons.

First, the valuations investors place on shares are exogenous to the model: divergent beliefs are not explained. Second, such divergence would appear to imply that a "winner's curse" should always be observed. If those placing the highest values on securities have typically overestimated their values, then participating in securities markets must, on average, be a losing proposition: one buys only those shares for which one has overestimated their values. Investors should, in fact, recognize this and update or adjust their estimates of value accordingly.

The problem of how investors form expectations of value for securities is a fundamental issue in finance and information economics. Any process in which expectations are formed must be subject to a test for rationality and consistency with the equilibrium concept. In common values auctions, for example, a "winner's curse" cannot be a part of any reasonable equilibrium. Since "winning the auction" (or "obtaining shares in the IPO") is itself an informative event, the willingness of bidders to pay various prices for a security is itself conditional on those prices being market equilibrium prices. For this reason the demands of investors for securities cannot in general have the simple form of consumers' demand curves for goods. This serious complication is lacking in Miller's analysis although, admittedly, many of these issues were formally analyzed years after Miller's contribution. Whether divergence of opinion can explain first day returns when expectation formation is rational and consistent with market equilibrium remains an open question worth investigating.[49]

One of the oldest and most straightforward heterodox explanations for underpricing, tangentially related to Baron's (1982) principal-agent formulation, is the monopoly or market power theory. In this view, underwriting is regarded as cartelized, with investment bankers enjoying a privileged, monopoly position with respect to issuers. The banks exploit this power by forcing issuers to accept low offer prices. Investors who are profitable, regular customers of the underwriters and their affiliated brokers receive allocations and reap excess returns. The underwriters are willing to enforce this paradoxical cash give-a-way because they then recoup these excess returns in the form of high trading fees and commissions from favored customers.

Several theoretical and empirical objections can be raised to the market power explanation of underpricing. First, why do underwriters engage in this complex charade of recycling profits from monopoly in one market (underwriting and distribution) into profits from another, perhaps competitive market (financial services)? Would it not be simpler and more efficient to merely take IPO profits directly in the form of higher fees and larger gross margins from underwriting? Second, if brokerage customers have access to numerous potential service providers, why don't they "take the money and run," enjoying excess IPO returns today and selecting a cheaper broker tomorrow? While such behavior might lose them future favorable allocations in IPOs, that is irrelevant when service fees consume excess returns. If the fees do not consume all the excess returns, then the underwriter is giving money away merely to affect the recycling of monopoly profits.

On the empirical side, there is little evidence that underwriting and/or distribution exhibit monopoly. The competitive nature of underwriting has some confirmation (Hays (1971), Hays (1979)). Evidence from antitrust suits do not support the notion of cartelization (Medina (1953)). Finally, Beatty and Ritter (1986) produce strong evidence that excessive mispricing by underwriters is punished by a loss of market share. Hence, the monopoly power hypothesis has not proven to be a credible explanation of early excess returns.

We turn finally to the notion, popular in many early analyses of mispricing, that excess returns merely reflect risk aversion on the part of one or another market participant. Note first that risk aversion is, in fact, an integral part of many conventional theories of underpricing: the Grinblatt and Hwang (1989) signalling model requires risk aversion on the part of the issuer, for example. We are interested here, though, in the idea that risk aversion is, by itself, a sufficient explanation.

It is important to distinguish between any underpricing motives created by risk aversion and the general IPO comparative static conclusion, found in almost all models, that increases in uncertainty over issue value are associated with greater underpricing. Increases in uncertainty can affect issuer and investor behavior (even when all parties are risk neutral) by, for example, exacerbating adverse selection. Yet, this observation is quite distinct from the claim that risk aversion itself explains underpricing.

Early suggestions that risk aversion is a primary explanation of underpricing frequently assume market power on the part of underwriters: Bear and Curley (1975) is a representative example. Given a risk averse underwriter who has purchased a block of shares in a firm commitment offering, uncertainty over market reception of the issue may lead to underpricing as a form of insurance. It is certainly true that IPO share prices are risky and highly volatile. Whether this explanation is theoretically credible is doubtful, however. Since investors would typically risk only a tiny fraction of their collective wealth on the issue, it is unclear why they must be "bribed" by inflated returns to accept it. Further, whatever risks investors are being compensated for must be highly transitory: excess returns after the first day of trading are rare, and the long run performance of IPO securities is either average or poor. Further, while excess returns exist on average for IPOs, about half of all IPOs produce negative returns (Ibbotson (1975)), and only the extreme skewness of returns produces the overall positive result.

The great degree of underpricing exhibited by the smaller, more speculative best efforts offerings also undermines the risk aversion explanation. Unlike a firm commitment contract, a best efforts offering imposes much less risk on underwriters since they do not commit themselves to purchase any shares. Since no insurance is provided to the issuer, underpricing would seem anomalous.

OTHER IPO MODELS

While underpricing has been the main object of research on IPOs, a number of other issues have also attracted the attention of investigators. The purpose of this section is to briefly review some of this theoretical literature with an eye toward explaining the underlying ideas and, perhaps, fostering additional work on some worthy topics. As will become obvious, several of the topics we investigate here are related to the underpricing puzzle, although they all involve additional issues often ignored in models of IPO pricing.

Among the topics investigated to date are the choice of offering type (best effort vs. firm commitment), the determination of offer provisions such as over-allotment and minimum sales constraints, the levels of bid-ask spreads for IPO securities, the use of outside certification by underwriters, accountants, or venture capitalists, and intertemporal patterns of IPO returns.

The choice of offer type is perhaps the most obvious ancillary problem in the analysis of IPO performance. Most models of underpricing, when they make any assumption at all, assume a firm commitment offering form. Yet it is clear that firm commitment and best efforts offerings exhibit important empirical differences, and that the theoretical analysis of these offer types is likely to proceed along different lines. Unlike a firm commitment contract, a best efforts offering bestows no insurance benefits on the issuing firm. The underwriter doesn't actually underwrite the issue, but instead provides only a distributional and advising role. From the issuer's point of view, one important characteristic unique to best efforts offerings is the possibility of failure.[50] On the empirical side, statistical evidence shows that best efforts offerings tend to be smaller, riskier, and more underpriced on average.

Bower (1989) offers a game-theoretic analysis of the choice of offering type consistent with many of the stylized facts about best efforts offerings. Bower's analysis does not address the initial underpricing phenomenon, and focuses instead on the cost and return consequences to issuers of different offering types. The issuer's problem is to maximize proceeds from the offering and a later sale of retained shares. Risk aversion plays no direct role in the analysis. The choice of offering method affects both the cost of funds and investor perceptions of firm value.

Formally, the firm requires an investment of \$I to realize a project with a random return X where $\underline{X} < X < \overline{X}$, and $\underline{X} > I$. The project cash flow X is known to the firm, yet investors know only the distribution of returns f(X). The firm sells a percentage p of its shares to the public in an IPO. The price of the share sold is then just (I/p). The issuer maximizes retained firm value $[X - C_i] (1 - p)$, where C_i is the cost of issuing shares by method i, and i represents the offer type: $i = B$ is a best efforts offering, $i = F$ is a firm commitment contract. Without loss of generality, let $C_B = 0$, $C_F = C$.[51]

If the owner uses a firm commitment contract, the expected value NPV_F of the owner's position is $NPV_F = [X - C] (1 - p)$. Suppose the underwriter, by diligent investigation, learns X and reveals this information to investors. Then investors pay the investment cost I in exchange for a portion of the firm having value I. Hence we must have $p [X - C] \geq I$. Thus, the net present value of the project is just $NPV_F = X - I - C$.

This analysis has several implications. First, some low X firms have a negative net present value of the owner's share under a firm commitment offering. This arises whenever $X < I + C$. On the other hand, a best efforts offering may always have a positive present value to the owner if $\underline{X} > I$. The complicating factor, though, is the valuation placed by investors on shares in a best efforts offering. By selecting such an offering type, owners reveal information on their project value X though underwriters provide no certification of this value. The willingness of any firm to go public in best efforts fashion depends on the resulting assessments of firm value by investors. Thus we seek a rational expectations equilibrium in which: (1) firms of sufficiently high value use a firm commitment contract; (2) lower value firms use a best efforts offering; (3) investors have accurate beliefs about the values of firms using one or another offering; and (4) at least some firms with a positive net present value under a firm commitment contract utilize a best efforts offering. Equilibrium is characterized by a project value y, $\underline{X} < y < \overline{X}$, such that all firms with values below y utilize a best efforts offering, and all firms with values above y choose a firm commitment contract.

The model has several plausible implications for firm behavior. First, increased underwriting costs C lead to fewer firm commitment offers, a result consistent with Ritter (1984), who documents an inverse relationship between offer proceeds and the probability of a firm commitment contract. Second, the separation properties of equilibrium -- in which high value firms utilize firm commitment offerings -- is consistent with most observations. Finally, Bower's analysis suggests that while share retention should be positively related to firm value in a firm commitment offering, no such link should exist in best efforts situations.

Although Bower's model does not address initial underpricing, the results may shed light on the problem of why best efforts offerings are often severely underpriced. The existence of a set of informed investors who know firm value in the best efforts cases may necessitate underpricing in the manner suggested by Rock (1986). The lack of value certification in best efforts offerings may exacerbate the adverse selection phenomenon visited on uninformed investors.

The analysis of Sherman (1992) on the pricing of best efforts offerings provides additional insights on the offer selection problem. Sherman views best efforts offerings as allowing the issuer and investors to make contracts conditional on market reception of the issue. Underpricing, as in Benveniste and Spindt (1989), is disguised compensation for the costly information acquisition efforts of investors. When information is discouraging, the cancellation options afforded by the best effort format are valuable to the issuer. By making an offer contingent on market reception, the uninformed issuer is able to take advantage of relevant information privately held by potential investors.

Our analysis of the selection of offering type highlights the fact that there are many provisions of an "institutional" nature that may be important in explaining IPO behavior. Related to the issue of offer type selection is the problem of introducing clauses in the contracts consummated by issuers and investment bankers. In particular, best efforts offerings often make use of "minimum sales constraints" (MSCs), legal provisions which void the offer unless a minimally acceptable sales target is obtained. Firm commitment offerings, on the other hand, often incorporate "over allotment options" (OAOs) which allow sales of additional shares in the event of sufficient oversubscriptions in the initial offering. These common institutional features, which are not incorporated in most models of underpricing, are analyzed by Welch (1991).

The introduction of MSCs and OAOs presumably serve various purposes, some of which are probably only tangentially related to underpricing. MSCs, for example, may well reflect strict minimum capital requirements arising for some investment projects. Despite this, MSCs and OAOs may have profound effects on the extent of underpricing realized in an offering. Welsh examines the implications of MSCs and OAOs for underpricing in the models of Benveniste and Spindt (1989) and Rock (1986), and presents some empirical evidence. He finds support for the Benveniste and Spindt model, but only mixed results for the adverse selection formulation. In any event, a formal analysis of MSC and OAO provisions represents a worthwhile direction for future research.[52]

When IPO securities trade in over-the-counter markets, bid-ask spreads may reveal valuable information on the natures of the securities (Glosten and Milgrom (1985), Ho and Stoll (1980)). Received theory suggests that bid-ask spreads reflect the marginal costs of being a dealer, and these costs arise primarily from the costs of holding inventories and the risks associated with trading with better informed agents. Theoretical work has thus far failed to provide a model of bid-ask spreads aimed directly at IPO securities, yet the evidence of Hedge and Miller (1989) suggests that the determinants of these spreads differ between IPO and seasoned instruments. If, for example, the informed/uninformed trader dichotomy of adverse selection models is accepted, trades in IPO securities may expose dealers to enormous risks arising from adverse selection. Thus, the spreads in these markets may in fact be related to the level of underpricing.

A number of authors have examined the role of certification in IPO performance, and our previous discussions of the adverse selection and signalling models touched on this idea. The analysis of certification has often been linked to various models of under-pricing (especially Rock (1986)); yet certification itself is neither an explanation of, nor an automatic remedy for, underpricing. Rather, certification can be thought of as a combination of an independent assessment of value or financial soundness, and a kind of insurance policy possibly according disgruntled investors a right to sue with some meaningful chance of recovering damages. To the degree that certification actually removes investor uncertainty about share value, then high value firms are likely to seek certification while low quality firms avoid it. Beatty and Ritter (1986), Booth and Smith (1986), Carter and Manaster (1990), Johnson and Miller (1988) and Megginson and Weiss (1991) offer various examinations of the certification hypothesis.

We turn finally to theoretical explanations for secular variations in the average levels of IPO initial returns, the so-called "hot issues" market problem. A number of authors (Ritter (1984), Ibbotson (1975), and Ibbotson and Jaffe (1975)) have observed the existence of short (e.g., 18-month) periods characterized by high numbers of offerings exhibiting very large initial returns. The periods 1959-1961, 1968-1969, and 1980-1981 serve as examples. In the period January, 1980 through March, 1981, Ritter (1984) found average first-day returns of 48.4%, an extraordinary performance even by IPO standards. This return stands in contrast to a "paltry" 16.3% initial return for the rest of the 1977-1982 period. Explaining the occurrence of such "hot issue" markets is a fundamental problem in IPO research.

Most researchers who have attempted to explain hot issues markets have built their explanations on one or another of the main theoretical models used to explain underpricing. While most such models are not dynamic, a comparative statics analysis of the effect of "exogenous" changes on the degree of underpricing in such models may provide a useful starting point for a dynamic approach. In this view there is, in fact, nothing inherently dynamic in IPO pricing: what one observes is a sequence of temporary equilibria which exhibit different levels of underpricing due to changes in background factors such as investment opportunities or market risks. A hot issue market is merely some equilibrium that exhibits sufficiently high underpricing, and the nature of previous equilibria have no explicit role to play in explaining current performance.

Two examples of this sort of theorizing will suffice to identify the main issues involved. Ritter (1984) utilizes the Rock adverse selection model (as of then unpublished) to examine the hot issues market of 1980-1981. As discussed previously, one implication of Rock's analysis is that increases in ex ante uncertainty over issue value necessitate increases in underpricing. Hence, highly uncertain issues are more underpriced. Ritter uses this and other implications of Rock's model in an attempt to explain the 1980-1981 market. In particular, if Rock is correct, then one expects that IPOs during the 1980-1981 period would exhibit greater value uncertainty than in other periods. Ritter's findings, however, are not particularly supportive of Rock's hypothesis. Ritter finds that almost all of the hot issue results were attributable to natural resource sector IPOs, implying market segmentation or some other sort of inefficiency. Further, these results coincide with a very high run-up in the values of seasoned natural resource issues trading on major exchanges.

In a similar spirit, Allen and Faulhaber (1989) suggest that hot issues markets may represent "temporary equilibria" that exhibit separation and underpricing. Utilizing a signalling model that exhibits both pooling and separating equilibria, Allen and Faulhaber argue that changes in background parameters related to firm cost and profitability factors can trigger changes from no underpricing, pooling equilibria to separating equilibria that exhibit underpricing. This interesting suggestion is likely to be difficult to empirically test, however, due to the challenges of finding suitable proxies for some relevant model parameters.

Relatively little formal analysis of hot issues markets is available. In one sense this is unsurprising. Because there is not unanimous agreement on the proper explanation for underpricing, it is to be expected that explanations for changes in the levels of underpricing will obtain even less consensus. One difficulty, which has not been the subject of any formal modeling, is the extent to which hot issues markets (and the secular patterns of IPO returns generally) really are an inherently dynamic phenomenon. If IPO returns through time merely represent a series of "independent" events, then static models of pricing may be sufficient. Notions of market "efficiency" may even seem to imply the necessity of such a temporally disaggregated view. Yet the possible existence of actual intertemporal dependencies may be admissible. Could not the performance of one IPO influence the expectations of investors and others about a later IPO? Could not the firms base their decisions to issue shares on the receptions comparable offerings experienced? Although such linkages seem plausible and even likely, models of this sort remain to be formulated.

5. TESTING THEORIES OF UNDERPRICING

INTRODUCTION

The previous chapter provides an extensive review of the main theories so far proposed to explain underpricing. The primary "orthodox" explanations -- adverse selection, principal-agent relationships, and signalling by issuers -- all suggest that underpricing arises as a rational, equilibrium response to some important informational asymmetry between market participants. Additionally, some competing "heterodox" explanations, such as those proposed by Benveniste and Spindt (1989) and Welch (1992), also posit differentially informed agents to explain this puzzling phenomenon. Given the large number of rigorous, well specified explanations for underpricing, one wonders which explanation comes closest to the truth. This question is the subject of this chapter.

It must be admitted at the outset that testing theories of underpricing, and distinguishing between them, is a very difficult problem. Several factors contribute to the onerous nature of this enterprise. First, as is usually the case in the social sciences and business, available data is nonexperimental. Any information provided by observed market behavior necessarily arises from a process about which the researcher knows all too little. While econometric techniques are formulated precisely in response to the problem of analyzing such data, lack of experimental controls implies that a certain unavoidable residual of uncertainty must be attached to all conclusions. The reader should bear this in mind.

A second significant difficulty in distinguishing between theories arises due to the consistent agreement between many theories over the determinants of underpricing levels.

For example, the models of Rock (1986), Baron (1982), and Grinblatt and Hwang (1989), all suggest a positive relationship between the degree of investor uncertainty over issue value and the extent of underpricing. Hence, evidence of a positive correlation between initial returns and some value uncertainty proxies (such as offer size), while interesting, does not allow the researcher to distinguish between competing theories.

A third difficulty for empirical testing of underpricing theories arises from the nature of the models themselves. In virtually all cases, asymmetric information is not directly observable, but instead must be inferred from certain observable magnitudes available for study. This implies that any test is likely to involve an additional, untested assumption: the variables selected to represent the level of informational asymmetry must successfully do so if the test is to be valid, or else one must find implications of the theories which imply certain distinct relationships between observable variables.

As a result of the complications described above, empirical testing of underpricing theories has followed two dissimilar paths. The first path attempts to find proxy variables for important model characteristics such as the level of informed trading in an IPO. The success of such an approach clearly depends on the success in selecting proxies. A second path, which is somewhat more in the modern spirit, eschews proxy variables and restricts analysis to tests of certain equilibrium conditions between observable magnitudes implied by the models. While this second approach is probably methodologically preferable, research is by definition limited to evaluation of only a small subset of most model predictions. In a general sense, of course, both approaches are necessary and, one hopes, ultimately complementary.

Prior to reviewing empirical tests of specific theoretical models, we turn first to a brief treatment of a body of literature which attempts to evaluate the link between share value uncertainty and the degree of underpricing. As noted above, the evaluation of this link does not provide a useful way to distinguish between various theories: almost all theories suggest that stocks with very uncertain values will be more underpriced on average. It appears probable, in fact, that this uncertainty-underpricing connection is itself a stylized fact about IPOs which is used in guiding theoretical model building. This link is nevertheless of some independent significance and has served as a focus of much early empirical research on IPO underpricing.

Among the papers which have examined, at least in passing, the link between value uncertainty and underpricing are: Ederington (1974), Bear and Curley (1975), Beatty and Ritter (1986), Miller and Reilly (1987), Johnson and Miller (1988), and Carter (1992). Almost all such analyses utilize a "proxy" approach to measuring value uncertainty. A wide range of such proxies has been proposed, including aftermarket price volatility, issue size, and the number of uses of offer proceeds given in the prospectus. Presumably aftermarket price volatility, small issue size, and numerous uses for offer proceeds imply greater uncertainty over value, although such a link is not explicitly drawn. Further, the distinction between risk and value uncertainty is often not formally made.

With these above-mentioned caveats, empirical analyses have uniformly shown that greater uncertainty over values is associated with greater levels of underpricing. This result is robust both to changes in the historical eras selected for analysis and to changes in the proxies used to represent this uncertainty. While this result constitutes an important fact about IPOs, we have seen that a positive correlation between value uncertainty and underpricing is a consequence of most theoretical models, and therefore does not allow us to distinguish between them.

TESTS OF UNDERPRICING THEORIES

We turn now to a critical review of the main empirical tests of the IPO underpricing models described in the previous chapter. For reasons of space and consistency, we will limit our investigation to those empirical papers which most directly address the problems of testing the models: ancillary results, which have but slight bearing on the theoretical models, are mostly omitted. As we shall see, evidence for most theoretical models is mixed, and considerable investigation remains to be done.

As noted in the previous chapter, Kevin Rock (1986) suggests that underpricing arises as a compensation device for uninformed traders. The existence of informed traders implies that uninformed traders receive shares in IPOs with greater frequency when the shares are "bad" (overpriced) than when they are "good." In order to attract the uninformed to the market, shares must be underpriced on average.[53]

Rock's model has several implications for market performance that facilitate testing using both the "proxy" and "equilibrium condition among observable variables" approaches. First, the level of informed trading should be positively correlated with underpricing. Any device that guarantees reduced informed trading should increase prices and reduce initial returns. Second, the method by which shares in oversubscribed offerings are rationed is critically important, and should be related to underpricing in a way to be explained below. Most importantly, equilibrium implies only normal returns (no rents) to uninformed traders. Informed traders -- who bid only on underpriced issues -- presumably make (potentially large) profits, although these profits may, in a broader view, serve as compensation for the costs of becoming informed (Beatty and Ritter, (1986)). In addition to these features, the Rock model has a number of other equilibrium implications that are not obviously usable for testing proposes.[54]

The role of informed trading in determining the level of underpricing has been the basis for several "proxy"-style tests of Rock's mechanism. The "bias" against uninformed traders arises from two intertwined features: the uninformed have a bigger chance of receiving bad shares (since the informed do not bid on them), and the rationing rule used to allocate shares in-oversubscribed offerings gives inadequate, or no, preference to uninformed traders. Rock's original analysis assumed purely random rationing independent of investor type and order size. Such purely random schemes do not correspond very closely with actual rationing practices, to be described below. In particular, though, the role of underwriters and their syndicates in distributing issues may be important in determining the level of underpricing because the way shares are rationed directly affects the probabilities with which various types of investors receive allocations. Further, characteristics of the underwriters may convey information to investors on the extent of informed trading.

Several studies have evaluated the roles of underwriter characteristics and allocation rules in determining the levels of underpricing. Unfortunately, underwriter characteristics (such as "prestige") may convey (signal) information on both the level of informed trading and unobserved IPO security characteristics such as "riskiness." It seems more plausible that underwriter prestige signals security quality rather than the level of informed trading. In any event, Beatty and Ritter (1986), Carter (1992), and Carter and Manaster (1990), offer interesting insights on this issue. In general, high prestige underwriters underprice their securities less than other underwriters.

McStay (1992) utilizes British data to evaluate the Rock model. Adopting the distributional analysis of Kenny and Klein (1983), McStay argues that investment banks reduce underpricing by preferentially allocating shares to "uninformed" customers. Curiously, these uninformed traders are assumed to be active private investors having close relationships with distributing brokers. In the U.K., IPOs are of two main types: the "offer for sale" and the "placement." The former impose strict random allocation rules similar to the assumptions made by Rock (1986), while the latter resemble U.S. IPOs in allowing the underwriter wide discretion in distribution. Hence, if the preferential allocation notion is correct, one expects less underpricing in placements than in offers for sale. Of course, offers for sale and placements differ in other ways (e.g., in the allowable minimum sizes of the offers); so an uncritical comparison is not useful.

McStay attempts to estimate the levels of uninformed demand by noting that, in general, the demand for "bad" IPOs must primarily consist of uninformed buyers. Technical complications aside, any valid estimates of uninformed demands should allow one to construct "theoretical" portfolios for uninformed traders. The question then becomes "is the expected return to the uninformed trader zero?" McStay presents some evidence in support of this proposition, although considerable caution should be applied to these results for statistical reasons discussed by McStay.

Koh and Walter (1989) also turn to markets outside the U.S. in an effort to evaluate Rock's model. In particular, Singapore imposes strict rationing rules on oversubscribed offerings. Further, and happily for the analyst, rationing is public: the probabilities of getting shares is known. Koh and Walter argue that, if one weights share allocations by rationing probabilities (assuming the uninformed invest in all IPOs, being unable to tell the good from the bad), one should get a portfolio offering only a normal return.

Koh and Walter's analysis provides perhaps the strongest statistical evidence in support of the Rock model. Specifically, they find that: (1) expected returns to the uninformed portfolio are normal;[55] (2) the greater the degree of oversubscription of the offering, the greater the level of initial returns; and (3) results (1) and (2) are robust to various partitions of the data set based on issue and/or underwriter sizes. This is especially strong evidence in support of Rock's model because it seems highly unlikely that the returns to a portfolio of IPO securities, constructed along the lines described above, would exhibit zero excess returns unless Rock were right.

"Static" type tests of Rock's model, utilizing the equilibrium condition that uninformed traders receive only a normal return, provide some credible evidence in support of the adverse selection mechanism. As mentioned in the previous chapter, however, Rock's model is less successful in explaining secular variations in the average levels of underpricing, i.e., the "hot issues" problem (Ritter (1984)). However, it is clear from our previous discussion that underpricing increases not only in response to increases in uncertainty over share value, but also in response to changes in the levels of informed trading. This latter factor is, of course, considerably more difficult to empirically analyze insofar as investor type is not generally observable. Yet, the data of Koh and Walter (1989), or the technique for estimating uninformed trading proposed by McStay (1992), may provide an opportunity to reexamine hot issues markets using information on changes in the levels of informed trading in addition to offering value uncertainty proxies. Such an analysis, which would constitute an important test of the generality of Rock's idea, has not yet been undertaken.

The principal-agent analysis of Baron (1982), which may be considered as a rigorous outgrowth of the older "monopoly" view of underwriting, suggests that underpricing occurs due to attempts by the issuer to motivate the agent (underwriter) both to expend effort on sales promotion activities, and to reveal private information valuable to the issuer. Thus, underpricing arises in this framework because the investment bank has private information unavailable to the issuing firm.

Baron's analysis focuses on the nature of the optimal contact between the issuing firm and the underwriter. Analysis of this sort is notorious for producing complex results which may defy rigorous testing. Yet, the basic informational asymmetry assumed by Baron -- bankers know more than issuers -- can be exploited to produce a clever test of Baron's insight. In particular, investment banks sometimes "go public" in an IPO which they "self-market." In such cases there is no separation of issuer and underwriter; so no informational asymmetry of Baron's type can arise. Hence, if Baron is correct, one would expect zero systematic underpricing in these special IPOs. Muscarella and Vetsuypens (1989) use this approach in evaluating Baron's model. They examine 38 IPOs of investment banks which participated in the distributions of their own securities over the years 1970-1987. Muscarella and Vetsuypens find that, contrary to the "predictions" of the Baron framework, these IPOs exhibit statistically significant underpricing, with first day returns of around 7% on average. Further, the prestige of the investment banks appears insignificant in explaining the degree of underpricing. While the Muscarella and Vetsuypens data set is small, their results cast considerable doubt on the importance of issuer/underwriter information asymmetries in explaining underpricing.

The idea that underpricing arises from attempts by issuers (underwriters) to signal their private information on the values of shares is developed in theoretical models by Allen and Faulhaber (1989), Grinblatt and Hwang (1989), Welch (1989), and others. The logic here is that issuers know more about share value than do any other market participants. Issuers with high value projects would like to prove this to investors. Underpricing can either be a signal of value, or may establish the reliability of some more traditional signal such as share retention.

Testing "signalling models" is a difficult proposition. First, there are a number of such models, and these models are not strictly comparable with one another. The order of moves, the informational environment, and other critical theoretical characteristics, differ between models. Second, most signalling models admit multiple equilibria, some of which involve "pooling" (no signalling), so one might say that signalling models explain "too much" to be confidently tested.[56] Finally, while the nature of the asymmetric information assumed in signalling models is quite modern in spirit, the distinctive predictions of signalling models usually can be tested only by evaluation of both initial <u>and</u> longer holding period returns. Since underpricing shares is costly, signalling makes sense only if the issuer retains shares for later sale in a seasoned offering. It is returns from these later sales that "justify" the earlier signalling. Yet many IPOs are one shot: no further sales of shares are made.[57] For these and other reasons, statistical tests of signalling models of underpricing are few and far between.

The general idea that informed insiders signal firm value characteristics to outside investors is widely known and frequently tested in the formal literature of finance. IPOs, due to their special characteristics, probably afford both an inviting, and treacherous, natural experiment for evaluating the signalling idea. Downes and Heinkel (1982) provide an important early application of the share retention signal suggested by Leland and Pyle (1977) to a sample of 297 larger, U.S. IPOs for the period 1965-1969. Downes and Heinkel regress firm market values on the offered value of the IPOs and α, the proportion of shares retained by the owners (utilizing the transformation $\hat{\alpha} = \alpha + \ln (1 - \alpha)$). Several estimation techniques and data formulations are utilized, and the role of dividends as value signals is also investigated. Downes and Heinkel find that share retention levels are significantly and positively associated with firm value in the manner suggested by Leland and Pyle (1977).

Ritter (1984) offers a useful comment on the Downes and Heinkel (1982) methodology by proposing stronger empirical tests and competing alternative hypotheses for the share retention -- market value linkage. Noting that share retention may be positively correlated with firm market value for several largely unrelated reasons, Ritter provides additional empirical evidence using a sample of 559 U.S. IPOs for the period 1965-1973. Ritter's findings cast doubt on the Downes and Heinkel results: the percentage of shares retained is not seen as a significant determinant of firm market value. Indeed, Ritter's results appear more supportive of an "agency" interpretation for this linkage in which managerial shirking <u>alters</u> firm values.

It is important to recognize that the Leland and Pyle signalling hypothesis does not explain IPO security underpricing. Extensions of the Leland and Pyle framework to the underpricing problem, e.g., Grinblatt and Hwang (1989), allow one to derive a set of potentially testable implications. In particular, the Grinblatt and Hwang analysis suggests that:

(i)   Given D, α and σ^2 are negatively related;
(ii)   Given α, V is positively related to σ^2;
(iii)   Given σ^2, V is positively related to α;
(iv)   Given V, α is negatively related to σ^2.

Here α is percentage of shares retained, V is true firm value (revealed in the aftermarket), D is the pricing discount, and σ^2 is the variance of (unspanned) firm cash flows. As a reading of the previous chapter shows, these results are broadly consistent with Leland and Pyle's analysis. Further, the Grinblatt and Hwang model suggests some additional, new testable propositions:

(v)   Given α, D increases as σ^2 increases;
(vi)   Given σ^2, D increases as α increases;
(vii)   Given α, V is positively related to D;
(viii) Given σ^2, V and D are positively related.

Grinblatt and Hwang (1989) point out that empirical results offered by Ibbotson (1975), Ibbotson and Jaffe (1975), Beatty and Ritter (1986), Chalk and Peavy (1987), Ibbotson, Sindelar and Ritter (1988), and Hwang (1988), often tend to confirm at least some of these theoretical findings, although none of these empirical papers is designed as an out-and-out test of their model. Clearly substantial additional empirical analysis is needed.

The lawsuit avoidance theory of Tinic (1988) has been the subject of two empirical evaluations, one offered by Tinic and the other by Welch (1991). Tinic notes that the Securities Act of 1933 greatly expands the opportunities for disgruntled investors to pursue lawsuits against the underwriters of underperforming IPOs. Tinic utilizes data from IPOs for the years 1923-1930 and 1966-1971 to evaluate excess return behavior. Tinic finds that:

(i)   Underpricing is much greater in the later years (post 1933);

(ii)   Prior to the Securities Act of 1933, there is no relationship between underpricing and investment banker reputation;

(iii)   After 1933, prestigious underwriters begin to shun highly speculative issues, leading to the currently observed "segmented" market in underwriting services.

These results provide at least approximate support to Tinic's theory, although numerous institutional changes in the financial markets between the sample years studied by Tinic make one reluctant to give unqualified support to Tinic's conclusions.

Tinic's analysis of pre-1933 data is as important for gaining insights into other theories of IPOs as it is in testing the lawsuit avoidance theory. Tinic finds underpricing of IPOs in the 1920s; yet the levels of discounting observed are only about 5%, far less than modern studies indicate. Clearly, underpricing was less severe sixty years ago than it is today. Explaining this result, which is in some ways akin to explaining the "hot issues" problem, would appear to present difficulties for some theories of IPO pricing discussed in the previous chapter. Further investigation of early financial data is warranted.

Welch (1991) provides an interesting empirical examination of some common contract provisions observed in IPOs. Best effort offerings frequently incorporate "minimum sales constraints" that allow withdrawal of the offer if it is poorly received. In firm commitment offerings, over-allotment options allow the underwriter to sell additional shares when demand is sufficiently robust. Welch's main purpose is to examine the use of these contract provisions in the theoretical frameworks provided by Benveniste and Spindt (1989) and Rock (1986); yet Welch provides some evidence of the Tinic lawsuit avoidance hypothesis. In particular, Welch finds that "riskier" firm commitment offerings are associated with greater underwriter compensation. Yet, the number of risk factors for which underwriters can be held liable (listed on the prospectus) is unrelated to underpricing levels. However, the Tinic theory suggests that underpricing should rise as these legal liability risk factors increase in number. Thus, one concludes that under-writers are compensated underlinedirectlyunderline for risky offerings, not underlineindirectlyunderline through the insurance explicit in underpricing.

Although the proxy used for underwriter liability risk is almost surely imperfect, Welch's results are not supportive of Tinic's theory of underpricing. Ideally, one would wish to examine data on actual lawsuits and the liabilities of underwriters to confidently pass judgment of Tinic's insight.

Welch (1991) has as a primary purpose an examination of the underwriter preselling model of Benveniste and Spindt (1989). Benveniste and Spindt use game theory to model preselling activities by underwriters. When a potential investor has favorable private information on the offering's prospects, the investor must be given a proper incentive to reveal it since such information can lead to higher initial prices. In order to secure truthful reporting by potential investors, the underwriter designs a "revelation mecha-nism" that induces investors with favorable information to share their insight with the underwriter. This is achieved by offering preferential allocations of shares to investors reporting good information. Such a scheme works because lying (e.g., reporting discouraging news when indications are favorable) reduces the chances of getting an allocation of shares which are probably good. Repeated interaction between underwriters and knowledgeable investors helps to support this cooperation.

The Benveniste and Spindt model has several implications, only some of which are directly testable. First, "regular" investors should get preferential treatment in allocations, a conclusion with much anecdotal support. Second, when investor information is more valuable, underpricing should increase. Further, underpricing should be positively related to the level of presales and premarket interest. Note especially the contrast between this model and that of Rock (1986): in Rock, informed investors are a burden on issuers, not a helpful source of valuable information.

Welch (1991) evaluates the Benveniste and Spindt mechanism by examining the implications of this mechanism for underpricing in the presence of over-allotment and minimum sales clauses. In particular, if Benveniste and Spindt are correct, then one expects that: (1) over-allotments options should reduce underpricing by making it easier to preferentially treat regular investors with good news; (2) minimum sales constraints should increase underpricing; and (3) underwriters should be compensated for accepting high minimum sales requirements and low over-allotment options.

Welch empirically tests these predictions using data on 363 best efforts offerings and 660 firm commitment offerings of U.S. companies for the period 1977-1982. Proxies for offer riskiness and other environmental factors are utilized in a sophisticated regression format. Welch finds that the data support the Benveniste and Spindt (1989) theory: high minimum sales constraints and lower over-allotment options cause underwriters to force more of the offering in the presale, leading generally to the efforts outlined above.

The incomplete spanning argument of Mauer and Senbet (1992) is informally evaluated by the authors using a large sample of 1002 U.S. IPOs from the period 1977-1984. Mauer and Senbet's theoretical analysis suggests that: (1) underpricing should be unrelated to systematic risks (beta); (2) underpricing levels increase in the variance (dispersion) of the unspanned component of IPO security cash flow; (3) industries should exhibit different levels of underpricing since they presumably exhibit different degrees of secondary market spanning; and (4) underpricing should be reduced for later issues in a given industry as spanning by previously issued securities increases. To test these propositions, Mauer and Senbet analyze returns by three digit S.I.C. code industry groups and find substantial inter-industry variation in returns, a result echoing Ritter (1984). Proxies for investor access to the primary market (offer size), issue riskiness (Dimson (1979) market model regression results), and other variables are analyzed in a regression format. Results are generally supportive of the model's theoretical predictions, although a heavy reliance on proxy variables is present. Clearly, however, average IPO performances differ between industries, a fact that presumably requires some explanation.

6. Conclusion

Initial public offerings play a crucial role in allocating resources in market economies. By accessing external sources of funds through an IPO, the new firm is able to acquire that capital necessary for firm growth and product innovation. Equity financing may be particularly attractive for "high risk" entrepreneurial ventures, and such enterprises represent an important motive force of economic development.

Because of the enormous importance of IPOs, understanding how IPOs work is a fundamental part of understanding financial markets generally. It is clear, however, that IPO markets involve unique features unobserved in any other important financial markets. In particular, the recurring and puzzling existence of enormous average first day returns to equity IPOs in the U.S. and other countries has long been recognized as an anomalie of the first order. Explaining these returns in a theoretically rigorous way is one of the primary problems of financial economics.

Many theoretical models of IPO underpricing, in addition to being ingenious, offer an appealing way to become acquainted with some of the most important ideas in modern microeconomics and finance theory. Such generally useful concepts as adverse selection, moral hazard, signalling, and information sharing assume central roles in several modern theories of underpricing. The purported lesson of each of these applications is, of course, that underpricing, while appearing anomalous, is actually just an equilibrium phenomenon illustrating some surprising consequence of rational behavior in a suitably peculiar environment.

Despite the considerable intellectual work expended on the "IPO problem," it does not appear that a single, universally valid explanation for IPO pricing is at hand. While it is perhaps quite unrealistic to ask for so much from any one theory, science must always prefer "simple" theories of wide applicability over complex models which only seek to explain some isolated phenomena. Put this way, it is apparent that much remains to be done in modeling IPO markets.

Most theorizing and discussion of the IPO problem has, at least implicitly, adopted the view that underpricing is a result of rational behavior and, further, that this mechanism is most explicable when IPOs are viewed "in isolation." No feature of the extant literature is more striking than the dearth of work on any truly dynamic model of IPOs. While a number of excellent empirical studies have evaluated secular patterns in IPO returns (e.g., Ritter (1984), Ritter (1991), Ibbotson (1975)), we lack any comprehensive studies that seek to relate returns across IPOs through time. In particular, there is no model that explains why the success (or failure) of an IPO at time t might be relevant to the performance of some other IPO at time t + 1. Is it, or is it not, plausible that IPO returns might be correlated in this way? To the extent this linkage is just the old notion of "market ebullience," one might be tempted to dismiss the entire issue. Yet it seems unlikely that investors learn nothing from the performances of previous IPOs.

A related issue, addressed indirectly by papers such as Mauer and Senbet (1992), concerns the role, if any, of IPO industry characteristics in determining the levels of "mispricing." Mauer and Senbet (1992) and Ritter (1984) both find some evidence of the importance of industry characteristics in determining the level of underpricing. Clearly, uncertainty over issue values is critical: Anderson, Born, and Beard (1991) find no underpricing for closed-end investment company equity IPOs, essentially sales of repackaged financial assets. Presumably industry characteristics vary in ways that affect the ability of outside investors to accurately value IPO shares. Further, market reception of one IPO in an industry may reveal information on investor sentiment relevant to the success of later IPOs in the same industry.

The above discussion suggests the following classification scheme. Seller specific information relevant to valuing an IPO might be of (at least) three types. First, information specific to the issuing firm, including its prospects and the competence of its management, is clearly valuable to investors. Information of this sort is the type most often analyzed in theoretical models of IPOs, but is by definition useless for valuing other IPOs. Second, investors may obtain information relevant to the industry or sector in which the IPO occurs. In this case, reception of one IPO might provide information on the prospects of later IPOs in the same industry. Third, information may be of a general sort so that the reception of one IPO is informative about the prospects of others in various sectors.

Empirical evidence that something like the above classification scheme is operative is not hard to find: Mauer and Senbet (1992) and Ritter (1984) provide examples. Such effects, however, are not well understood, and research in this area may represent an important direction for future activity. The consequences of all this for dynamic modeling of IPOs is obvious.

Lost in the theoretical maze of underpricing models are two additional issues of social concern: the income distributional consequences of IPO allotment behavior and the effects of underpricing as a "tax" on going public with an equity issue.

It is widely believed that the distribution of oversubscribed shares gives preference to "insiders," particularly in the U.S. McStay (1992) notes that, in the context of a Rock type adverse selection model, biases in share distributions can improve efficiency when "insiders" correspond to "uninformed" traders. This occurs because preferential treatment of uninformed traders reduces the underpricing necessary to secure uninformed participation in the offering. While it might be unrealistic to believe the preferred (i.e. profitable) customers of brokerages are uninformed in this sense, consideration of this issue clearly raises the problem of how shares are actually distributed, an issue about which little is known. Since the distribution scheme may affect the levels of underpricing selected, there is a social interest in the form distribution takes.

Further, the degree to which distribution mechanisms could be judged "fair" is hardly even mentioned in the extant literature. While "fairness" is a normative idea to be sure, it is not unimportant just because it is normative.

We note finally that the existence of large average discounts in most equity IPOs acts as a kind of tax on firms seeking to raise investment capital in the equity markets. This tax is enormous, representing almost 14% on average for a typical issue. When the discounts are viewed as taxes on issuing firms (taxes which are paid to investors instead of the government), one expects to see a variety of effects familiar from the analysis of the welfare consequences of taxation. In particular, larger discounts imply: (1) smaller issues; (2) fewer firms going public; (3) excessive reliance on debt financing; and (4) diminished inventive activity. All of these effects are probably deleterious in the long run. Further, evidence suggests that smaller issues exhibit even greater underpricing, suggesting that the "tax" is especially burdensome on small firms.

Understanding the IPO mechanism will likely remain a core problem for financial economics. The importance of venture capital and new business start-ups elevates the IPO discount phenomenon to an issue of nontrivial social concern. The value of insight into this problem is not reduced by the difficulties borne in obtaining it.

BIBLIOGRAPHY

Affleck-Graves, J., S. Hedge, R. Miller, and F. Reilly. "The Effect of the Trading System on the Underpricing of Initial Public Offerings," *Financial Management* (Vol. 22, No. 1, Spring, 1993): 99-108.

Aggarwal, R. and P. Rivoli. "Evaluating the Costs of Raising Capital Through an Initial Public Offering," *Journal of Business Venturing* (Vol. 6, 1991): 351-361.

Aggarwal, R. and P. Rivoli. "Fads in the Initial Public Offering Market?" *Financial Management* (Vol. 19, No. 4, Winter, 1990): 45-57.

Aggarwal, R., R. Leal, and L. Hernandez. "The Aftermarket Performance of Initial Public Offerings in Latin America," *Financial Management* (Vol. 22, No. 1, 1993): 42-53.

Allen, F. and G. Faulhaber. "Signaling by Underpricing in the IPO Market," *Journal of Financial Economics* (August, 1989): 303-323.

Anderson, S. and J. Born. "The Selling and Seasoning of Investment Company Offerings," *Journal of Financial Services Research* (Vol. 2, 1989): 115-131.

Anderson, S. and J. Born. "Other-Country Funds: IPO, Seasoning, and Post-Seasoning Return Behavior," *Journal of International Finance* (Vol. 2, Number 2, Spring, 1992): 103-114.

Anderson, S., J. Born, and R. Beard. "An Analysis of Bond Investment Company IPOs: Past and Present," *The Financial Review* (May, 1991): 211-222.

Archer, S. and L. Faerber. "Firm Size and the Cost of Externally Secured Equity Capital," *The Journal of Finance* (Vol. 21, No. 1, March, 1966): 69-83.

Balvers, R., B. McDonald, and R. Miller. "Underpricing of New Issues and the Choice of Auditor as a Signal of Investment Banker Reputation," *The Accounting Review* (Vol. LXIII, No. 4, October, 1988): 605-622.

Baron, D. "A Model of the Demand for Investment Banking Advising and Distribution Services for New Issues," *The Journal of Finance* (Vol. 37, No. 4, 1982): 955-976.

Barry, C and R. Jennings. "The Opening Price Performance of Initial Public Offerings of Common Stock," *Financial Management* (Vol. 22, No. 1, Spring, 1993): 54-63.

Bear, R. and A. Curley. "Unseasoned Equity Financing," *Journal of Financial and Quantitative Analysis* (Vol. 37, 1975): 311-325.

Beatty, R. and J. Ritter. "Investment Banking, Reputation, and the Underpricing of Initial Public Offerings," *Journal of Financial Economics* (Vol. 15, No. 1/2, Jan-Feb, 1986): 213-232.

Benveniste, L. and P. Spindt. "How Investment Bankers Determine the Offer Price and Allocate New Issues," *Journal of Financial Economics* (October, 1989): 343-361.

Block, S. and M. Stanley. "The Financial Characteristics and Price Movement Patterns of Companies Approaching the Unseasoned Securities Market in the Late 1970s," *Financial Management* (Winter, 1980): 30-36.

Bolino, A. *The Development of the American Economy.* 2nd ed. (Columbus: Charles E. Merrill Publishing Co., 1966).

Booth, J. and R. Smith, II. "Capital Raising, Underwriting, and the Certification Hypothesis," *Journal of Financial Economics* (Vol. 15, No.1/2, Jan-Feb, 1986): 261-281.

Bower, N. "Firm Value and the Choice of Offering Method in Initial Public Offering," *Journal of Finance* (Vol. 44, No. 3, 1989): 647-662.

Brennan, M. "Latent Assets," *The Journal of Finance* (Vol. 45, No. 3, 1990): 708-730.

Brimmer, A. "Credit Conditions and Price Determination in the Corporate Bond Market," *Journal of Finance* (Vol. 15, September, 1960): 353-370.

Brown, J. "Post-Offering Experience of Companies Going Public," *Journal of Business* (Vol. 43, January, 1970): 10-18.

Buckland, R., J. Herbert, and K. Yeomans. "Price Discount on New Equity Issues in the UK and Their Relationship to Investor Subscription in the Period 1965-1975," *Journal of Business Finance and Accounting* (Vol. 8, No. 1, 1981): 79-95.

Carter, R. "Underwriter Reputation and Repetitive Public Offerings," *The Journal of Finance* (Vol. 15, No. 4, Winter, 1992): 341-354.

Carter, R. and S. Manaster. "Initial Public Offerings and Underwriter Reputation," *The Journal of Finance* (Vol. 45, No. 4, 1990): 1045-1067.

Chalk, A. and J. Peavy, III. "Initial Public Offerings: Daily Returns, Offering Types and the Price Effect," *Financial Analysts Journal* (September-October, 1987): 65-69.

Chalk, A., and J. Peavy, III. "Understanding the Pricing of Initial Public Offerings," *Research in Finance* (Greenwich, CT: JAI Press, 1990).

Chemmanur, T. "The Pricing of Initial Public Offerings: A Dynamic Model with Information Production," *The Journal of Finance* (Vol. 48, No. 1, 1993): 285-304.

Cho, S. "The Possibility of Failure and the Pricing of Best-Efforts Initial Public Offerings," *Quarterly Review of Economics and Finance* (Vol. 32, No. 2, 1992): 30-45.

Conard, J. and M. Frankena. "The Yield Spread Between New and Seasoned Corporate Bonds, 1952-1963." in *Essays in Interest Rates* pp. 145-222. Edited by Jack Guttentag and Phillip Cagen. (New York: Columbia University Press, 1969).

Dimson, E. "Risk Measurement When Shares are Subject to Infrequent Trading," *Journal of Financial Economics* (Vol. 40, March, 1985): 105-124.

Downes, D. and R. Heinkel. "Signaling and the Valuation of Unseasoned New Issues," *The Journal of Finance* (Vol. 37, 1982): 1-10.

Drake, P. and M. Vetsuypens. "IPO Underpricing and Insurance Against Legal Liability," *Financial Management* (Spring, 1993): 64-73.

Ederington, L. "The Yield Spread on New Issues of Corporate Bonds," *The Journal of Finance* (Vol. 29, 1974): 1531-1543.

Fung, W. and A. Rudd. "Pricing New Corporate Bonds Issues: An Analysis of Issue Cost and Seasoning Effects," *The Journal of Finance* (Vol. 41, 1986): 633-642.

Gale, I. and J. Stiglitz. "The Informational Content of Initial Public Offerings," *The Journal of Finance* (Vol. 44, 1989): 469-477.

Geisst, C. *Visionary Capitalism.* (New York: Praeger Publ., 1990).

Glosten, L. and P. Milgrom. "Bid, Ask, and Transaction Prices in a Specialist Market with Heterogeneously Informed Trades," *Journal of Financial Economics* (Vol. 14, March, 1985): 71-100.

Grinblatt, M. and C. Hwang. "Signalling and the Pricing of New Issues," *The Journal of Finance* (Vol. 44, No. 2, 1989): 393-420.

Grossman, S. and J. Stiglitz. "On the Impossibility of Informationally Efficient Markets," *American Economic Review* (Vol. 70, No. 3, June, 1980): 393-408.

Hayes, S. III. "Investment Banking: Power Structure in Flux," *Harvard Business Review* (March-April, 1971): 136-152.

Hayes, S. III. "The Transformation of Investment Banking," *Harvard Business Review* (January-February, 1979): 153-170.

Hedge, S. and R. Miller. "Market-making in Initial Public Offerings of Common Stocks: An Empirical Analysis," *Journal of Financial and Quantitative Analysis* (Vol. 24, 1989): 75-90.

Ho, T. and H. Stoll. "On Dealer Markets Under Competition," *The Journal of Finance* (Vol. 35, May, 1980): 259-268.

Hughes, P. and A. Thakor. "Litigation Risk, Intermediation, and the Underpricing of Initial Public Offerings," *Review of Financial Studies* (Vol. 5, No. 4, 1992): 709-742.

Hwang, Chaun Yang. "Signalling In a New Issue Market" (UCLA Doctoral Dissertation, 1988).

Ibbotson, R. and J. Jaffe. "'Hot Issue' Markets," *The Journal of Finance* (Vol. 30, No. 4, 1975): 1027-1042.

Ibbotson, R. and J. Ritter. "Initial Public Offerings," in *Handbook of Operations Research and Management Science: Finance* (North Holland, 1991).

Ibbotson, R. "Price Performance of Common Stock New Issues," *Journal of Financial Economics* (No. 2, 1975): 235-272.

Ibbotson, R., J. Sindelar, and J. Ritter. "Initial Public Offerings," *Journal of Applied Corporate Finance* (Summer, 1988): 37-45.

Jog, V. and A. Riding. "Underpricing in Canadian IPOs," *Financial Analysts Journal* (November-December, 1987): 48-55.

Johnson, J. and R. Miller. "Investment Banker Prestige and the Underpricing of Initial Public Offerings," *Financial Management* (Summer, 1988): 19-29.

Kenny, R. and B. Klein. "The Economics of Blockbooking," *Journal of Law and Economics* (Vol. 26, 1983): 497-540.

Koh, F. and T. Walter. "A Direct Test of Rock's Model of the Pricing of Unseasoned Issues," *Journal of Financial Economics* (Vol. 23, No. 2, August, 1989): 251-272.

Leland, H. and D. Pyle. "Information Asymmetries, Financial Structure, and Financial Intermediation," *The Journal of Finance* (Vol. 32, No. 2, 1977): 371-387.

Levis, M. "The Long-Run Performance of Initial Public Offerings: The UK Experience 1980-1988," *Financial Management* (Spring, 1993): 28-41.

Levis, M. "The Winner's Curse Problem, Interest Costs and the Underpricing of Initial Public Offerings," *The Economic Journal* (Vol. 100, March, 1990): 76-89.

Lindvall, J. "New Issue Corporate Bonds, Seasoned Market Efficiency and Yield Spreads," *The Journal of Finance* (Vol. 32, No. 4, 1977): 1057-1067.

Loderer, C., D. Sheehan, and G. Kadlec "The Pricing of Equity Offerings," *Journal of Financial Economics* (No. 29, 1991): 35-57.

Logue, D. "On the Pricing of Unseasoned Equity Issues: 1965-1969," *Journal of Financial and Quantitative Analysis* (Vol. 8, No. 1, January, 1973): 91-103.

McBain, M. and D. Krause. "Going Public: The Impact of Insiders' Holdings on the Price of Initial Public Offerings," *Journal of Business Venturing* (No. 4, 1989): 419-428.

McDonald, J. and A. Fisher. "New-Issue Stock Price Behavior," *The Journal of Finance* (Vol. 27, 1972): 97-102.

McDonald. J. and B. Jacquillat. "Pricing of Initial Equity Issues: The French Sealed-Bid Auction," *The Journal of Business* (Vol. 47, No. 1, January, 1974): 37-47.

McKenna, C. *The Economics of Uncertainty.* (New York: Oxford University Press, 1986).

McStay, K. *The Efficiency of New Issues Markets.* (New York: Garland Publishing, Inc., 1992).

Mauer, D. and L. Senbet. "The Effect of the Secondary Market on the Pricing of Initial Public Offerings: Theory and Evidence," *Journal of Financial and Quantitative Analysis* (Vol. 27, No. 1, 1992):55-79.

Medina. H. Corrected Opinion of Judge Medina: U. S. vs. Henry Morgan et al, Civil Action No. 43.757, District Court of the United States for Southern New York, 1953.

Megginson, W. and K. Weiss. "Venture Capitalist Certification in Initial Public Offerings," *The Journal of Finance* (Vol. 46, No. 3, 1991): 879-903.

Miller, Edward M. "Risk, Uncertainty, and Divergence of Opinion," *The Journal of Finance* (Vol. 32, No. 4, 1977) 1151-1167.

Miller, R. and F. Reilly. "An Examination of Mispricing, Returns, and Uncertainty for Initial Public Offerings," *Financial Management* (Summer, 1987): 33-38.

Muscarella, C. "Price Performance of Initial Public Offerings of Master Limited Partnership Units," *The Financial Review* (Vol. 23, No. 4, November, 1988): 513-521.

Muscarella, C. and M. Vetsuypens. "A Simple Test of Baron's Model of IPO Underpricing," *Journal of Financial Economics* (Vol. 24, No. 1, September, 1989): 125-135.

Myerson, R. *Game Theory: Analysis of Conflict* (Cambridge: Harvard University Press, 1991).

Nanda, V. "Why Firms Go Public," unpublished working paper, University of Chicago, 1988.

Neuberger, B. and C. Hammond. "A Study of Underwriters' Experience with Unseasoned New Issues," *Journal of Financial and Quantitative Analysis* (Vol. 9, No. 2, March, 1974): 165-177.

Neuberger, B. and C. LaChapelle. "Unseasoned New Issue Price Performance on Three Tiers: 1975-1980," *Financial Management* (Vol. 12, 1983): 23-28.

Peavy, J. "Returns on Initial Public Offerings of Closed-End Funds," *Review of Financial Studies* (Vol. 3, No. 4, 1990): 695-708.

Rasmussen, E. *Games and Information.* (Cambridge: Basil Blackwell Publishers, 1994).

Rees, R. "The Theory of Principal and Agent: Part 1," *Surveys in the Economics of Uncertainty* (New York: Basil Blackwell, 1987).

Reilly, F. "Further Evidence on Short-Run Results for New Issue Investors," *Journal of Financial and Quantitative Analysis* (Vol. 1, January, 1973): 83-90.

Reilly, F. "New Issues Revisited," *Financial Management* (Vol. 6, Winter, 1977): 28-42.

Reilly, F. and K. Hatfield. "Investors' Experience with New Stock Issues," *Financial Analysts Journal* (Sept-Oct, 1969): 73-80.

Ritter, J. "The 'Hot Issue' Market of 1980," *The Journal of Business* (Vol. 57, No. 2, 1984): 215-240.

Ritter, J. "Signaling and the Valuation of Unseasoned New Issues: A Comment," *The Journal of Finance* (Vol. 34, No. 4, 1984): 1231-1237.

Ritter, J. "The Long-Run Performance of Initial Public Offerings," *The Journal of Finance* (Vol. 46, No. 1, 1991): 3-27.

Rock, K. "Why New Issues are Underpriced," *Journal of Financial Economics* (Vol. 15, No. 1/2, Jan-Feb, 1986): 187-212.

Ross, S. "The Economic Theory of Agency: The Principal's Problem," *American Economic Review* (Vol. 63, 1973): 134-139.

Schwartz, R. *Equity Markets: Structure, Trading and Performance* (New York: Harper & Row Publ., 1988).

Shaw, D. "The Performance of Primary Common Stock Offerings: A Canadian Comparison," *The Journal of Finance* (Vol. 26, No. 5, December, 1971): 1101-1113.

Sherman, A. "The Pricing of Best Efforts New Issues," *The Journal of Finance* (Vol. 47, No. 2, 1992): 781-790.

Smith, C. "Investment Banking and the Capital Acquisition Process," *Journal of Financial Economics* (Vol. 15, No. 1/2, Jan-Feb, 1986): 3-29.

Sobel, R. *Inside Wall Street.* (New York: Norton & Co., 1977).

Spence, A. "Job Market Signalling," *Quarterly Journal of Economics* (Vol. 87, August 1973): 355-379.

Stoll, H. and A. Curley. "Small Business and the New Issues Market for Equities," *Journal of Financial and Quantitative Analysis* (September, 1970): 309-322.

Sutton, D. and W. Benedetto. *Initial Public Offerings: A Strategic Planner for Raising Equity Capital* (Chicago: Probus Publishing Co., 1988).

Tinic, S. "Anatomy of Initial Public Offerings of Common Stock," *The Journal of Finance* (Vol. 43, No. 4, 1988): 789-822.

98

Titman, S. and B. Trueman. "Information Quality and the Valuation of New Issues," *Journal of Accounting and Economics* (No. 8, 1986): 159-172.

Wang, K., S. Chan, and G. Gau. "Initial Public Offerings of Equity Securities: Anomalous Evidence Using REITs," *Journal of Financial Economics* (Vol. 31, 1992): 381-410.

Weinstein, M. "The Seasoning Process of New Corporate Bond Issues," *The Journal of Finance* (December, 1978): 1343-1354.

Weiss, K. "The Post-Offering Price Performance of Closed End Funds," *Financial Management* (Autumn, 1989): 57-67.

Welch, I. "Seasoned Offerings, Imitation Costs, and the Underpricing of Initial Public Offerings," *The Journal of Finance* (Vol. 44, No. 2, 1989): 421-449.

Welch, I. "An Empirical Examination of Models of Contract Choice in Initial Public Offerings," *Journal of Financial and Quantitative Analysis* (Vol. 26, No. 4, December, 1991): 497-518.

Welch, I. "Sequential Sales, Learning and Cascades," *The Journal of Finance* (Vol. 47, No. 2, June, 1992): 695-732.

Werner, W. and Smith, S. *Wall Street* (New York: Columbia University Press, 1990).

White, W. "The Structure of the Bond Market and the Cyclical Variability of Interest Rates," *International Monetary Fund Staff Papers* (March, 1962): 104-147.

ENDNOTES

1. Data taken from section "New Securities Issues" in Federal Reserve Bulletins for years 1940-1994

2. Werner, Smith, pp. 3,14

3. Adapted from Bolino, pp.213-217

4. Sutton, Benedetto, p.3

5. Werner, Smith, p.143

6. Bolino, p.217

7. Sobel, p.23

8. Sutton, Benedetto, p.3

9. Sutton, Benedetto, p.4

10. Bolino, pp. 360-363

11. Geisst, p.20

12. Review of the Regulation of Banking and Securities in Florida, Florida Senate Committee on Governmental Operations, March 1986, p.13.

13. Bolino, p.217

14. Geisst, p.12

15. Geisst, p.4. The National Bank Act of 1864 forbade banks from underwriting securities. After 1912, they circumvented the 1864 act by using affiliates.

16.   Schwartz, p.131

17.   Geisst, p. 3

18.   Securities Act of 1933, United States Securities and Exchange Commission, p.1

19.   Schwartz, p.130

20.   Schwartz, p.131

21.   Sutton, Benedetto, p.147

22.   Securities and Exchange Act of 1934, United States Securities and Exchange Commission, p.1

23.   Schwartz, p. 130

24.   In an earlier 1966 article "Firm Size and the Cost of Externally Secured Equity Capital," Archer and Faerber anticipate the size-effect theme in later IPO research in suggesting that small issues must be relatively underpriced in order to stimulate sales by underwriters.

25.   In an earlier study Brown finds that companies going public in "receptive" new issue markets are less likely to fail subsequently than those going public in a high cost "unreceptive" market environment.

26.   An earlier empirical piece by Shaw, "The Performance of Primary Stock Offerings: A Canadian Comparison," considered new stock offerings in the 1956-1963 period. This study focuses primarily on one through five year returns and finds that new issues essentially underperform seasoned issues.

27. Please see Ibbotson and Ritter (1990) which reports significant underpricing in foreign countries' IPOs found in earlier studies.

28. Earlier studies by Brimmer (1960), White (1962), and Conard and Frankena (1969) offer coupon differences, call provisions, and differential demand, respectively, as factors attributing to differences between new and seasoned issue yields.

29. For a discussion of information and investors see Grossman and Stiglitz (1980).

30. Readers familiar with game theory will recognize this as the "common knowledge" assumption. Rasmussen (1994) gives a readable overview.

31. For simplicity, most versions of the Rock model assume that informed investors have perfect information. This is not required, however.

32. McStay (1992) offers an interesting discussion that contrasts allocation roles in the U.S. and U.K.

33. This logic parallels early, "naive" theories of underpricing that explain low prices as representing demand uncertainty and risk aversion by issuers. We return to this theme below.

34. Beatty and Ritter actually analyze specific change in the distribution of values, a mean-preserving spread of a uniformly distributed variable. Similar analysis is used by Baron (1982). No one has investigated completely general changes in the distribution of value where, for example, an "increase in uncertainty over value" is represented as a

second order stochastic shift in the distribution, leading to a convex stochastic ordering in the variable returns.

35.   Though plausible, this assumption is not automatically true in all such circumstances. The degree of information gathering depends on the marginal benefits and marginal costs of information acquisition. McKenna (1986) offers a useful elementary discussion of search type problems.

36.   In a 1992 study Carter finds empirical support for the hypothesis that the likelihood of subsequent offerings is negatively related to IPO risk.

37.   Random variable x with distribution $f(x)$ is said to first-order stochastically dominate a variable y with cumulative distribution $G(y)$ if $F(c) < G(c)$ for any value c in the support of x and y. This implies x has a bigger mean than y, among other things.

38.   The principal's problem as stated here is simplified from that considered by Baron (1982). In particular, we ignore the decision by the principal over whether to make the offering or not.

39.   Moral hazard can arise whenever the agent can take an action which cannot be observed (and, hence, cannot be contracted on) by the principal, and the principal's and agent's interests diverge.

40.   See Brennan (1990) and Smith (1986) for interesting overviews on this phenomenon.

41.   Mixed equilibria, in which some agents reveal their types by their actions while others do not, are also possible.

42. The choices of auditor and investment banker as signals are modeled by Titman and Trueman in the 1986 article "Information Quality and the Valuation of New Issues."

43. Signalling models typically make an assumption of a fixed investment requirement. This restriction is probably far stronger than is first apparent. If variable levels of investment are possible, signalling may be impossible.

44. This is assumed so that retaining shares imposes a risk cost on the issuers, the issuers being unable to dispose of their remaining shares prior to the realization of x_1.

45. The 1989 article "The Informational Content of Initial Public Offerings" by Gale and Stiglitz develops a two-period model to consider the impact of having repeat sales of equity.

    In the 1993 article "The Pricing of Initial Public Offerings: A Dynamic Model With Information Production," Chemmanur develops an IPO pricing model wherein insiders sell equity both as IPOs and in the secondary market.

46. In a 1992 paper "Litigation Risk, Intermediation, and the Underpricing of Initial Public Offerings," Hughes and Thakor develop a formal model in which potential litigation can induce underwriters to sell an IPO at a price less than its assessed value.

47. Chalk and Peavy (1990) develop a model wherein investors receive IPOs in proportion to their consumption of other investment banker services. In this model underpricing is consistent with rationality on the part of issuers, bankers, and investors.

48. Welch (1989) offers some anecdotes.

49. The mere existence of differing opinions presents difficulties for theoretical analysis. If actions reveal private information, how can traders continue to have different opinions? In the jargon of game theory, can rational agents "agree to disagree?" See Myerson (1993) for a sophisticated discussion of this issue and the related problem of defining "common knowledge."

50. Cho (1992) offers a theoretical model of best efforts IPO pricing that explicitly recognizes the possibility of failure. About a third of all best effort offers fail.

51. Consider any costs incurred in both types of offerings as a component of I.

52. A similar issue arises in auction design with the use of minimum bid provisions. See Myerson (1993).

53. Note that informed traders must be unable to acquire sufficient capital to buy out a good issue, a capital market imperfection assumption.

54. For example, under some conditions one can show that the optimal discount is such that uninformed orders exactly equal the number of shares on offer. See McStay (1992) for details on this and several other "untestable" sorts of predictions.

55. "Normal" meaning comparable to the risk-free rate of return.

56. To the authors' knowledge, no econometric estimation of a multiple equilibrium signalling model using, for example,

finite mixture or switching regression techniques has ever been undertaken.

57.   Grinblatt and Huang (1989) offer some statistics on this issue.

INDEX